The Career Guide for
CREATIVE AND UNCONVENTIONAL PEOPLE

The Career Guide for
CREATIVE AND UNCONVENTIONAL PEOPLE

FOURTH EDITION

Carol Eikleberry, PhD, with Carrie Pinsky, MEd

Introduction by Richard N. Bolles

TEN SPEED PRESS
Berkeley

CE To Jerald Forster, my career mentor, for his kind heart, positive spirit, and steadfast support.

CP To Carol, who offers proof of the magical career connections that can happen when we take the time to meet a stranger for a cup of coffee.

Published in the United States by Ten Speed Press, an imprint of the
Crown Publishing Group, a division of Penguin Random House LLC, New York.
www.crownpublishing.com
www.tenspeed.com

Ten Speed Press and the Ten Speed Press colophon are registered trademarks
of Penguin Random House LLC.

Table on pages 28-29 reproduced by special permission of the publisher, Psychological
Assessment Resources, Inc., from *Making Vocational Choices*, copyright 1973, 1985, and
1992 by Psychological Assessment Resources, Inc. All rights reserved. Drawing on page
13 adapted from *Coming Alive from Nine to Five: The Career Search Handbook*, 2nd ed., copyright 1984 by Betty Neville Michelozzi. Used by permission of the publisher, McGraw-Hill.

Library of Congress Cataloging-in-Publication Data
Eikleberry, Carol.
The career guide for creative and unconventional people / Carol Eikleberry, Ph.D.,
with Carrie Pinsky, MEd ; introduction by Richard Nelson Bolles.—Fourth edition.
        pages cm
1. Vocational guidance. 2. Creative ability. I. Pinsky, Carrie, 1961- II. Title.

HF5381.E485 2015
331.702—dc23

        2015012026

Trade Paperback ISBN: 978-1-60774-783-3
eBook ISBN: 978-1-60774-784-0

Printed in the United States of America

Design by Anna Grace Adamczyk
Illustrations adapted from design by freepik.com

10 9 8 7 6 5 4 3 2 1

Fourth Edition

CONTENTS

ACKNOWLEDGMENTS

My first acknowledgment goes to Emeritus Professor Jerald Forster of the University of Washington, who suggested during a 1983 lecture on career counseling that someone should write a career book for Holland's Artistic types. In my mind's eye, all these years later, I can picture the spot where I sat in his classroom as I straightened up and thought: "What a good idea!" When I told him that I'd like to write such a book, he nurtured the project as my advisor, doing what he could within academe to support my goal. It was my great good fortune to be his student.

I'd like to extend special thanks to the following people whose work has greatly influenced this book: the editors, illustrators, and designers at Ten Speed Press, whose talents helped me turn my ideas into something you might actually want to read; Richard Bolles, for his amazing generosity and the model he provides in his book, *What Color Is Your Parachute?*; and John Holland, for an elegant and practical theory that gave me a new understanding of the work world and my place in it.

I'd also like to thank my husband, family, and friends. Many creative people, both clients and friends, shared with me their experiences and ideas and offered suggestions that improved the various editions of this book over the past twenty years. For their contributions to the fourth edition, I am particularly grateful to Lisa Cook, Bryan Dik, Rich Feller, Katy Piotrowski, and (most especially) Carrie Pinsky, my new co-author, who helped bring this edition into the digital age.

INTRODUCTION by Richard N. Bolles

Many, many books come across my reading table each year, but it has been a long time since one of them impressed me so much as this one has.

Carol has set out to illuminate a very perplexing subject—that of the creative or unconventional impulse in us all. And I found her insights quite dazzling. Chapter 2 alone is worth the price of the book.

I have found myself thinking again and again on some of the things she says. She has struck some deep chords with me.

The reason for this lies in the nature of language. Language is a marvelous invention, when you stop to think about it. Take the English language, for example. It uses just twenty-six symbols—which we call the letters of the alphabet—to describe everything. Millions and millions of things. All labeled or recalled with the aid of those twenty-six symbols.

A man named John Holland has gone the English language one better. He has invented an alphabet of just six symbols to describe more than twelve thousand occupations and their multiple job titles. John's alphabet has become the most popular system for describing occupations existing in the world today. More than thirty-five million copies of his Self-Directed Search, which enshrines that alphabet, have now been purchased and used by individuals to assess their personalities in order to determine suitable occupations.

The most significant difference between John's alphabet and the English alphabet, however, has nothing to do with numbers. It is the fact that in the English language the symbols themselves are used without any deep analysis of each symbol. In John's alphabet, the six symbols (A, S, E, I, R, and C) are fraught with meaning and significance, and they cry out for analysis. Over the years, that examination has been made, but it is safe to say that the least examined and least understood of John's alphabet—until now—has been the letter A, for Artistic.

Since A not only stands for a number of occupations, but also for a gift that potentially lies within us all—the creative impulse—the examination is long overdue.

Here are some of Carol's insights in this book that have particularly impressed me (I state them mainly as I have digested them, with a few in their pristine Carolinian form):

The essence of art or creativity lies in an unusual sensitivity to some aspect of everyday sensory experience, and this sensitivity is something we were born with.

The sensitivity is usually restricted to one area, rather than constituting sensitivity to everything.

The sensitivity may be to pictures, sounds, language, movement, human behavior, values (truth, honesty), or whatever. If you are not sure what your sensitivity is, "think about the kinds of ugliness that most distress you."

A person's particular sensitivity brings both pleasure and pain. "An artistic sensitivity to something combines the potential for a sublime experience with the agony of confrontation with the ordinary."

In going about their work, Artistic types prefer to use intuition, which looks for what the senses don't pick up and, most particularly, for the relationships among facts rather than just for the facts themselves.

This tends to lead them to awareness of what is wrong, within their arena of sensitivity. Therefore, creativity begins not with problem-solving, but with "problem-finding"—with the seeing or sensing of a problem. Creative people focus "on what is wrong, what is missing, what needs to be changed to make something better."

And while the emphasis is on problem-finding, as it turns out, "the way a problem is set up often suggests the resolution."

"Very often the Artistic person is an appreciator rather than a creator ... If it is hard to make your living by creating, it is doubly hard to make your living by appreciating."

This is just a sampler of the wealth of insights to be found in this book.

And what does all this have to do with job hunting? Well, in a highly competitive job market, often the key to success is first sitting down and thoroughly trying to understand yourself—before you go out there. Knowing who you are and what you have to offer is crucial. Carol has made an important contribution indeed to this self-understanding.

PART ONE

THE CAREER PROBLEM

"Money often costs too much."
—RALPH WALDO EMMERSON

"There's no money in poetry, but then there's no poetry in money, either."
—ROBERT GRAVES

Chapter 1
THE CAREER CHALLENGE

This book is your call to adventure. Your guide to adventure, too. If you want to have a creative career, you need to become the hero of your own life story.

Heroes set off on an adventure for one of two reasons: either change is forced upon them by unexpected life circumstances, like getting fired or divorced, or being assigned to the Boss from Hell; or else they are nudged into change from within, because of their own dissatisfactions. Maybe they're bored, or desperate to leave home, or they yearn to make a difference. However it comes, change is difficult.

Change is relentless, too. Sometimes it seems like our frenzied world of work is changing so fast that even superheroes will be swept off the face of the planet! Other times it seems like the village blacksmith model of employment is returning, as more people return to a private business venture that blends their work life with their home life. We're losing traditional job security and benefits in exchange for greater freedom and ownership of our work—except now our little "village" is vulnerable to global competition, staggering income inequality, and cataclysmic events occurring anywhere in the world.

What's a creative person to do?

Embark on your own career adventure!

This book will point the way to finding and following your own path. Your path may be fun at times—exhilarating, even—but it may not be easy or direct. Joseph Campbell, a famous scholar of the hero's journey, once put it: "If you can see the path laid out in front of you, step by step—it's not your path!"

That's why a creative career is an adventure. You've been told that treasure lies ahead . . . but to where is that map really leading? On a quest to find your personal workplace paradise, you will likely encounter conflict, setbacks, and discouragement. But you'll also find friendly allies, opportunities for personal growth, and a chance to bring more creativity into your life.

Ahhh. Creativity. Now that's worth taking some risks for. Creating can be so fun, so joyous, so naturally motivating and engaging that it feels more like play than work. Creating something new makes us happier and brings us more fully alive. This book promises to move you in that direction, so that your work becomes more creative and personally fulfilling.

But true creativity does not result from a few quick tips for your job search. Instead, it results from a deeply experienced spiritual quest to become the person you were born to become. The adventure begins when you set out to develop your own unique potential, instead of following conventional expectations to become like someone else. It is a hero's journey, undertaken not only to develop your own potential but also to return with a gift for the world.

I see you, my reader, in just this way—as the hero of your own life story. And I see myself as a guide for your journey. I have the appropriate credentials to be a mentor because I'm a psychologist who has studied creativity and career development from graduate school on. I also have relevant experience because I worked as a career counselor for more than twenty years. Furthermore, I have learned from readers of earlier editions of this book, who told me how stifled and unhappy and depressed they felt in jobs that provided no outlet for their creativity.

But there is one more reason that I feel qualified to be your guide: I've been there. I know how it feels to be underpaid and underemployed. An idealistic liberal arts major who never wanted to fit into the business world, I disliked most of my early jobs and burned out fast. I had a harder time finding work than my friends who went into accounting or engineering or sales, and I also made significantly less money than they did at first. I found it a lot easier to say what I didn't want to do than what I did want to do, but I knew that I wanted to use my brain, to have some autonomy, and to work on meaningful problems.

I have a special desire to help people who, like me, don't fit easily into conventional doctor or lawyer or banker molds. I wrote this book for people who want to keep learning and growing, who want to get paid for using their true talents at work, and who desire an opportunity for self-expression along with enough freedom to do things their own way instead of the way the work has always been done before.

I'd like to help make your career dreams possible—even if you are not yet sure exactly what your dream is—and to bring greater vitality to your experience of choosing or changing jobs. Think of me as your traveling companion, walking along beside you with a better knowledge of the territory ahead. I will share with you some maps created by my favorite trailblazers. By the end of the book, when we reach the end of our path together, you can continue on your own, with a newfound sense of adventure and more confidence in the creative unfolding of your own life.

Please note that some of the lists, questions, and other support tools you'll find in this book are available for downloading in the Career Notebook section of my website (www.creativecareers.com), so there's no need to write in the book. You can complete these on screen or print them out and fill them in, as you prefer. They can become part of your career notebook, described in detail in chapter 5.

AN OVERVIEW

Before we get started, let's begin with an overview provided by Lee Roy Beach, an emeritus professor and researcher on the subject of decision-making. I have used his Image Theory to organize this book.

According to Beach, we tend to make decisions as follows: first we survey the situation to figure out what's wrong, then we decide what we are going to do about it, and finally we take action. You go through a similar thinking process when you make a career decision:

First, you realize that you have a problem. Something is wrong. Maybe you need to make a career choice for the very first time. Or maybe you were laid off, or can't make ends meet. Perhaps you're troubled by a nagging desire to do something more meaningful with your life. This phase offers an opportunity to clarify any confusion you might feel and allows you to accept your responses as legitimate.

Next, you decide what you are going to do about the situation. What kind of work do you want to do? What are the possibilities? This is both an exciting and an uncertain time, as you look into lots of options, gather information from various sources, consider pros and cons, and learn about opportunities you never knew existed, in order to choose a new direction.

Finally, having made a choice, you make changes. You act on your values. This is usually the hardest part, because it requires giving up security and taking risks for something that may not work out. It also requires persistence, which does not come naturally to us human beings. We often say we are going to do something virtuous, like switch to a new and better occupation—but then fail to follow through.

As it turns out, Beach's model is both linear and circular, because you don't go through this process just once. It's currently predicted that younger workers will change jobs about fifteen times over the course of their careers; creative and unconventional people, with greater needs for change and variety, will probably change even more frequently than that. So you can expect to circle back through the process, again and again. You'll figure out what is wrong, set new goals, and then try to make them happen. And sometimes when you take action, you'll learn something new about yourself or the world of work that causes you to start over again.

So, I designed this book in three parts:

Part One is the "What's going on?" part. Here you will get a bird's-eye view of the world of work and learn how it is changing for the better. You will also be offered some insights on the creative personality. I hope this section will provide clarification and validation: you may have had trouble with your career for reasons that are no fault of your own, but employers have more reason than ever to value your creativity.

Part Two deals with career choice. It organizes an abundance of occupational possibilities, identifies a variety of potential employers, and suggests many different ways to arrange work in a creative lifestyle. Having all these options increases confidence and hope for the future. Yes, you can thrive as a creative person!

Part Three focuses on change and taking action. You'll find practical strategies for turning your dreams into reality and a vision of how your creative endeavors might help you grow as a person. Persistence, flexibility, and courage are highlighted, because they are as important as talent in the pursuit of fulfilling employment.

I wouldn't blame you for asking: Is fulfilling work even possible? A 2013 Gallup research survey found that 20 percent of employed persons in the United States pretty much hated their jobs, while another 50 percent felt disengaged.[1] And, those disgruntled 70 percent were among the lucky ones who had a job!

Economic security and job stability now sound as quaint and old-fashioned as Mom's apple pie. Some people can't find any paying work; others can't escape their entry-level job; others never get to stop working, putting in regular 60-hour weeks plus long commutes. Meanwhile, the ways that work is organized, conducted, and rewarded continue to transform. Globalization has created the most competitive job market in the history of the world. No wonder people feel miserable—but too scared to do anything about it!

But take heart. According to the Rockport Institute, "approximately 10 percent of people report that they love their work . . . When fit is optimal, workers find numerous indicators of increased job satisfaction, including experiencing work as a natural expression of one's talents and personality."[2] You could be in that fortunate 10 percent.

How do you move toward a job you love? Your first step is self-knowledge. We'll begin by looking at an elegant picture of the occupational world, using a theory developed in the twentieth century by renowned vocational psychologist John Holland. Research on Holland's theory, which has been conducted by researchers around the world for more than six decades, is devoted to helping people choose careers. In practice, Holland's theory has been so successful that it is now frequently used to organize career information in a wide variety of resources.

PERSONALITY TYPES

According to Holland's theory, there are six basic personality types in the world of work, and six corresponding work environments.[3] You are advised to go into a work environment that most closely fits your personality. So before you even start looking for work, assess your own personality to see which of the prototypes best describes you. You can begin right now, by comparing your interests to Holland's six model types.

The following interest checklist will give you a beginning idea of your personality type, according to Holland's framework. You can indicate interest in an occupation even if you don't know much about it and even if you don't have the skills or credentials required. You're not making any commitments now, just noting what you would like to do. Count the total number of checkmarks in each section and then compare across the sections to see where you have your greatest number. The two or three types with the greater numbers of checkmarks indicate your personality type. When you are finished, read the descriptions of Holland's six personality types that follow.

ARTISTIC

Actor	Dancer	Photographer
Architect	Editor	Singer
Blogger	Graphic designer	Sculptor
	Interior designer	___Total for Artistic

SOCIAL

Clergy member	Nurse	Social worker
Companion	Occupational therapist	Teacher
Counselor	Playground director	YWCA/YMCA director
	School principal	___Total for Social

ENTERPRISING

Executive	Manager	Salesperson
Funeral director	Politician	Stockbroker
Lawyer	Realtor	Supervisor
	Recruiter	___Total for Enterprising

INVESTIGATIVE

- Actuary
- Computer programmer
- Dentist
- Mathematician
- Optometrist
- Pharmacist
- Physician
- Research scientist
- Surveyor
- Veterinarian
- ___Total for Investigative

REALISTIC

- Farmer
- Forester
- Machinist
- Mechanic
- Pilot
- Plumber
- Police officer
- Rancher
- Repair person
- Soldier
- ___Total for Realistic

CONVENTIONAL

- Accountant
- Banker
- Cashier
- Clerk
- Computer operator
- Medical record technician
- Receptionist
- Secretary
- Tax preparer
- Telephone operator
- ___Total for Conventional

THE ARTISTIC TYPE (AKA CREATIVE AND UNCONVENTIONAL)

The Artistic type prefers unstructured work environments in which there is opportunity for self-expression. Artistic people describe themselves as being creative and unconventional and having ability with art, music, drama, or language. They like to solve problems by creating new products or processes. They are attracted to jobs in the fine arts, such as musician, actor, sculptor, dancer, or writer. However, they are also attracted to applied fields, such as commercial art, interior design, industrial design, journalism, and copywriting. Well-known Artistic types include Pablo

Picasso, Beyoncé, Chihuly, Usher, Donna Karan, Emma Stone, Lena Dunham, and Meryl Streep.

There is a great range along the Artistic spectrum, from people with great talent to those who appreciate the arts but don't believe they have any talent at all. Perhaps the luckiest possess a single talent that has been recognized and nurtured since childhood. Their path is pretty clear. But if you are not sure what your calling is, or if you have many talents that pull you in different directions, then it's harder to figure out what to do. In that case, knowing about your secondary interests may be helpful.

THE SOCIAL TYPE

The Social type is like the Artistic in that both types tend to be idealistic and in touch with their feelings. However, the Social type is more likely to prefer working with people. The Social person desires a work environment in which there is opportunity to train, heal, enlighten, or minister to others. They like to solve problems by helping others through feelings or intuition. They describe themselves as being understanding and popular and having ability in teaching and human relations. Social types are attracted to such jobs as teacher, minister, social worker, speech pathologist, nurse, and counselor. Well-known Social types include Mother Teresa, Oprah, Michelle Obama, and Joel Osteen.

THE ENTERPRISING TYPE

The Enterprising type is more like the Social than the Artistic. Both Social types and Enterprising types are sociable and skilled at communication and group leadership. However, the Enterprising person is more concerned about influencing or persuading than being helpful. Typically, Enterprising types have goals to make money or to run an organization. They like to solve problems by managing others and taking risks themselves. They may be entrepreneurial, creating new businesses. Enterprising types describe themselves as being dominant and confident and having ability in leadership and sales. They are attracted to jobs such as manager, director, executive, retailer, buyer, promoter, salesperson, and politician. Well-known Enterprising types include Arianna Huffington, Bill Gates, Hillary Clinton, Steve Jobs, Sophia Amoruso, and Warren Buffet.

THE INVESTIGATIVE TYPE

The Investigative type is like the Artistic in that both types are independent and introspective; they like to work with ideas and to work alone. However, Investigative people prefer a work environment in which there is opportunity to observe and analyze things in order to understand and predict them. Investigative types like to solve problems by thinking in abstract, analytical, task-oriented ways. They describe themselves as being scholarly and intellectual and having ability in science and math. They are attracted to jobs such as chemist, biologist, physicist, mathematician, physician, dentist, and research professor. Well-known Investigative types include Sanjay Gupta, Marie Curie, Albert Einstein, Brene Brown, Neil deGrasse Tyson, and Jane Goodall.

THE REALISTIC TYPE

The Realistic type is more like the Investigative than the Artistic. Like Investigative types, Realistic types like to work alone and to work with things; however, their work tends to be more concrete, such as manual work involving tools or machines. Less intellectually oriented than their Investigative counterparts, they prefer to solve problems by doing something physical with their hands or bodies. Many Realistic types are rugged, robust people who enjoy the outdoors. They describe themselves as athletic and mechanically inclined. They are attracted to jobs such as athlete, farmer, rancher, miner, soldier, plumber, electrician, and pilot. Well-known Realistic types include Serena Williams, Amelia Earhart, Tim Tebow, Captain Chesley Sullenberger, and Chris Kyle.

THE CONVENTIONAL TYPE

The Conventional type is, of all the types, the least like the Artistic. Artistic types prefer an unstructured work environment in which they can express themselves; Conventional types prefer an orderly work structure to which they can conform. Often Conventional types do the office work necessary to maintain an organization. Someone else initiates the task, and they responsibly carry it out, attending to every detail. They like to solve problems by following established procedures, especially procedures for organizing data. They have ability with numbers and clerical tasks. Their career choices include secretary, banker, accountant, cashier, tax expert, office manager, and computer operator. Because they tend to remain in the background, Conventional types rarely become well known, unless through an accident of birth or marriage, as in the case of Queen Elizabeth II or Pat Nixon.

So there you have them: Holland's six prototypes with examples of the work environments that best suit them. At this point, you might look back at the short interest test you took on page 8 and see how your answers compare to the six personality types described above.

Vocational psychologist Mark Savickas has some fun with the Holland types. He illustrates how the six types differ from each other by describing how each would approach the problem of a flat tire. Artistic types would cry or curse and then search for novel ways to change the tire. Social types would call up a friend and ask for help. Enterprising types would pay someone else to fix the tire. Investigative types would try to figure out what caused the flat; they might analyze the situation but not necessarily do anything about it. Conventional types would pull out the auto club cards they keep up-to-date and in the glove compartment. Only the Realistic types (theoretically, that is) would get out the appropriate tools and actually change the tire.

A hexagon best illustrates the relationships of the types to each other. The types closest to each other on the hexagon have the most in common; those across the hexagon from each other have the least in common. Artistic types usually share more interests with Investigative and Social types and have the least overlap with Conventional personalities. For example, Artistic and Investigative types share an interest in ideas; Artistic and Social types tend to be in touch with their feelings.

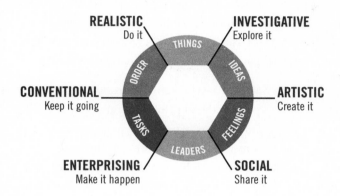

At this point, you're probably saying, "Gee, I see a little of myself in all of these types." You are right. Few people are truly pure types. Usually people identify two or three of the types as being most like them; sometimes they are more comfortable identifying the one or two types that are the least like them. You might ask yourself which two to four of the types you most closely resemble. For the remainder of this book, it will be useful to know which of the other Holland types, in addition to Artistic, best describe your personality. In my case, I know that I'm some combination of Artistic, Investigative, and Social, and that's precise enough for me.

John Holland developed the best test of his personality types, the Self-Directed Search (SDS). It is published by Psychological Assessment Resources. You can call the publisher at 1-800-331-TEST and ask them to mail you a sample pack (for about $24, including shipping). There are different forms of the SDS, so you might want to ask the publisher to help you pick the best form for you. Or you can take the most popular form of the SDS online at www.self-directed-search.com (for about $10).

The U.S. government also provides a test of Holland types, linked to their O*NET data about hundreds of occupations. For free, you can take an interest test that results in both your Holland code as well as matching occupations. The computerized version, called the Computerized Interest Profiler (CIP), can be found at www.onetcenter.org/CIP.html. The alternative test, taken with paper and pencil instead of a computer, is called the O*NET Interest Profiler (IP). This test is designed to be self-administered and self-interpreted. You will find a demo and PDF files for downloading everything you need at www.onetcenter.org/IP.html.

After you complete the Self-Directed Search or one of the O*NET interest profilers, you will know your three-letter Holland code, composed of the first letter of the three types you most closely resemble. For example, if you resemble Artistic the most, Social the next most, and Enterprising the next most after that, then your Holland code is ASE. You will also receive a list of the occupations most likely to appeal to someone with your interests. All these interest tests are quick, economical, and well-researched methods for starting your job search.

For many years I ran career groups for creative and unconventional people. Of all the activities in the group, the introduction to Holland's theory was voted the single most helpful by members of the groups. Here's what one group member wrote on an evaluation form:

> *"Oh, happiness! I'm greatly relieved to see that an unconventional, independent, creative person with original tendencies fits in some place on the globe. I worried that I didn't like to follow rules and preferred working alone, thought I was doomed to wander the earth unfulfilled and only partially happy."*

Just like that workshop member, many others have found Holland's theory truly helpful. If your Holland code is confirming and describes you well enough that you think, "This is who I am," that's great. However, not everyone is so enthusiastic. In fact, some readers have taken great offense, finding the Holland prototypes pejorative and even insulting. If you feel this way, please understand that the limitation lies with the theory. Although it is a good theory, it is only a theory and will never predict and perfectly explain a complex personality like your own.

If Holland's theory does not feel helpful to you personally, there is a simple alternative: instead of determining your Holland code, determine your interests. What are interests, anyway? I define them as those parts of reality on which you preferentially focus your attention. A simpler definition is that interests are what you like. For instance, what subjects would you like to learn more about? Remember, you can want to learn more even if you already know quite a bit about a subject. Although I know quite a bit about psychology, I am always eager to learn more about creativity and talent development, which are more specific interest areas within the field of psychology.

A field is an area of knowledge. If you went to college, you probably majored in a field. Fields are an easy way to identify your interests. Take a look at the following list (if you'd like a copy to use as a career choice support tool—one that you can print out and mark up—download the file from the Career Notebook section at www.creativecareers. com). Traditional creative fields are in boldface type. But if you are more interested in other subjects, there is no need to restrict yourself to traditionally creative fields. Since creative work involves ideas, and ideas can be about anything, any of the following fields could become a focus for your creativity.

Any person with any Holland code can be creative. Human beings are by their very nature creative. However, careers in the Artistic area tend to provide the best opportunity to be creative on the job. You'll be happy to know that your personality has not been defined to put you into a box, but to help you choose a fulfilling career. The theory moves directly from providing a handy label for your personality to identifying the kinds of occupations that would be most appealing to someone like you.

FIELDS

Advertising

Agriculture

Animal Care

Anthropology

Architecture

Art

Astronomy

Banking

Biology

Botany

Business Administration

Chemistry

Child Development

Civil Service

Communications

Computer Hardware
 and Software

Conservation

Construction

Corrections

Counseling

Crafts

Culinary Arts

Dance

Data Management

Defense

Dentistry

Design

Disabilities

Economics

Education

Electronics

Energy

Engineering

Environment

Fashion

Film

Finance

Foreign Languages

Foreign Service

Forestry

Foundations and
 Fundraising

Geology

Geography

Government

Health

History

Hospitality

Human Resources

Insurance

Journalism

Law

Law Enforcement

Library and Information
 Sciences

Literature

Marketing

Manufacturing

Mechanics

Medicine

Military Service

Mathematics

Multimedia

Museums and
 Historical Sites

Music

Nonprofit Organizations

Nursing

Organizational
 Management

Packaging

Personal Care and
 Fitness

Pharmaceuticals

Philosophy

Photography

Physics

Physiology

Politics

Printing

Psychology

Public Relations

Radio

Real Estate

Recreation and Leisure

Religion and Theology

Sales

Social Media

Social Work and
 Community Services

Sociology

Speech

Sports

Technology	Toys and Games	Utilities
Telecommunications	Translation and Interpretation	**Video** (including **Video Games**)
Television	Transportation	**Writing and Publishing**
Textiles	Travel	Zoology
Theater Arts		

FINDING A GOOD FIT

According to Holland's theory, work environments are also Artistic, Investigative, Realistic, Social, Enterprising, or Conventional. An Artistic work environment requires creative ability and rewards unconventional behavior, and it is dominated by Artistic types. Other work environments require and reward different abilities and behavior. Each of the six Holland work environments is dominated by workers of that type. Although there will always be variation in any occupational group, most accountants are Conventional, most sales managers Enterprising, most scientists Investigative, and so on.

This is useful information because, in career research, one consistent finding is that people like to work with people like themselves, people who share their interests, values, and abilities. As the saying goes, birds of a feather flock together. Many career counselors try to help their clients find flocks of the same feather. After assessing their clients' personality types, they suggest careers dominated by people of like type. Social types are encouraged to consider Social jobs, Artistic types Artistic jobs, and so on. Once you know which two to four types you most closely resemble, you can start looking at the occupations that appeal to people like you.

For example, the job of being a reporter is coded ASE, which means it is Artistic first, Social second, and Enterprising third. According to the theory, this job would be ideal for those whose Holland code is ASE. The Career Reference Section in the back of the book includes Holland codes for occupations whose first or second letter is A. All have components likely to appeal to people with an artistic or unconventional bent.

There's a lot to be said for choosing work that fits your personality. For one thing, research shows that if people choose work based on interests shared by coworkers, they are more likely to feel happy and successful at their jobs and less likely to make career changes later in their lives.

> "Designers are the new rock stars."
>
> —AMBRA MEDDA, DESIGN MIAMI BASEL

(The converse is also true: if people choose work in which their interests are unlike those of their colleagues, they are more likely to feel dissatisfied and to later switch to work more congenial to their personalities.) Research shows that a person's interests tend to be very stable—that is, they don't change much over time—so it makes sense to use your interests when making long-term decisions.

My own career history illustrates this point. For a while after college I worked as a waitress, and I was miserable. I was either bored out of my mind or stressed by having too many things to do at once. After waiting tables, I worked for a longer time as a receptionist in a doctor's office and found that better, but still unpleasant. The Holland code for waitress is CES and for receptionist is CSE—clear indicators that those jobs were not a good fit. Then Holland's theory helped me choose more suitable work, which provides a better overlap with my Artistic, Investigative, and Social—AIS—tendencies. The code for counseling psychologist is SIA, the code for career counselor is SAE, and the code for writer is AIE. You'll note that the three-letter match doesn't have to be perfect.

THE MISMATCH

Finding a career that fits your personality, therefore, seems reasonable and, relatively speaking, easy to achieve. In fact, it would be easy if there were enough matching jobs to go around. Unfortunately, the occupational world is not so ideal. In the United States, at least, the job market has been heavily biased toward the left side of Holland's hexagon. There have been many more Realistic and Enterprising jobs than Investigative, Artistic, and Social jobs.

Realistic, Conventional, and Enterprising types have been lucky, in that they have had more jobs to choose from and fewer people to compete with. Investigative and Social types have faced more competition, but their challenges were nothing like the competition for Artistic jobs. It has been harder for an Artistic type than for any of the other personality types to find matching work.

Historically speaking, Artistic jobs have been pitifully scarce: only about 1.5 percent of the U.S. civilian labor force was employed in Artistic occupations in 1990. At the same time, about 9 percent of American men and 13 percent of American women were classified as Artistic. This means that in 1990 there were about seven times as many Artistic types as there were Artistic jobs. If you were looking for creative work back then, the deck was stacked against you.

But there is good news. In the twenty-first century, there are proportionally more and more opportunities for people who want to do creative work. Although the creative role will probably always be a minority function in most cultures, the world of work has changed dramatically and promises to continue to change in ways that will benefit unconventional people. The workplace revolution of our time, fostered in part by the spread of the Internet and digital technology, promises ever greater opportunity and reward for creativity.

Here are some heartening trends from a book published in 2005:

> *"In the United States, the number of graphic designers has increased tenfold in a decade; graphic designers outnumber chemical engineers by four to one. Since 1970, the United States has 30 percent more people earning a living as writers and 50 percent more earning a living by*

composing or performing music. . . . More Americans today work in arts, entertainment, and design than work as lawyers, accountants, and auditors."[4]

The sea change in the world of work shows up in any number of publications. An entire issue of *Fast Company* magazine was devoted to the importance of design for success in business. A book about style claims ". . . the demand for style experts and aesthetic workers is clearly exploding."[5] A breakthrough book informs us that we are members of a new creative class that is fueling the world's economic growth.[6] Business writers employ the language of theater (for example, "getting into character") to suggest ways that businesses can compete, using theater arts as a model: "Companies stage an experience whenever they engage customers, connecting with them in a personal, memorable way."[7] Wherever you look these days, it appears that the business world appreciates the value of creativity and the arts. In fact, businesses are deliberately restructuring themselves in order to increase innovation!

Chapter 3 contains more information on changes that have taken place in the world of work—changes that offer hope for you. For now, you can comfort yourself with the knowledge that there is an increasing worldwide demand for creative services and products. Electronic technology has made it possible for anyone to join a mobile or off-site workforce, communicating with colleagues in different time zones, even different countries. As the conventional job with predefined roles and set hours disappears, the new work world presents great opportunities to unconventional people who are flexible, independent, and eager to learn.

PRACTICAL PROBLEMS

Although the future appears brighter and brighter, some very real and practical problems remain for unconventional people who want to do creative work. These problems, more than any other factor, prompted me to write this book. The growth of creative fields slowed after 2001,[8] and a mismatch was still evident in 2010,[9] with job instability and lower pay prevailing for many Artistic occupations, despite the hype.

Career counselors often find that Artistic types are the hardest kind of client to help because their interests don't generally point them toward secure and well-compensated employment. Classic Artistic jobs tend to be very competitive, despite less-than-average job security. Employment is often more volatile in creative fields, responding more dramatically than mainstream occupations to upturns and downturns in the economy.

A report of the employment and earnings of California's entertainment workforce revealed that about half of workers in the entertainment industry made their primary income from nonentertainment occupations. The majority of these workers did not have steady employment, but instead were hired on a project-by-project basis. Even though jobs were sporadic, there were still more entertainment workers than there were jobs.

The good news is that when they were employed, these entertainment workers earned higher wages than the state average, helping to compensate for periods of time without employment.[10] California is not unusual in that regard: in Australia, creative workers (with the exception of musicians and other performers) routinely earn above-average incomes.[11]

Calculating an average salary for many Artistic jobs can be much more difficult than determining the pay range for Conventional jobs such as an accountant or a nurse. Periodic employment is one complicating factor. Actors, for example, tend to work sporadically. According to the 2013–2014 Actors' Equity Association, off-Broadway stage actors' weekly salaries range from $566 to $1,008 per week, depending on the number of seats in the theater. But, when the show ends, so does the paycheck. Most actors are faced with the undeniable pressure of putting food on the table by taking odd jobs between shows while simultaneously auditioning to land their next creative opportunity.

Artists who earn a living marketing their wares often struggle with how to price their goods and pay themselves fairly. For example, painters, sculptors, and jewelry makers find it challenging to put a dollar value on their work. It is easy to add up the cost of their supplies, but how do they account for the time and talent necessary to create their unique products? How much should they earn per hour and what is a reasonable profit margin? This remains an artist's dilemma and contributes to the lack of predictable salary data for freelance artists.

Another challenge in terms of identifying salary expectations for Artistic careers is related to extreme variability and discrepancies in compensation. We know a local musician who earns about $75,000 per year playing weddings, bar mitzvahs, and other private parties. He also offers guitar and drum lessons during the week. He owns a home, supports a family, and enjoys a happy, creative life. But his earnings are a pittance when you consider that Bon Jovi raked in over $100 million in 2013. A talented public speaker may get paid $1,000 to $2,500 per gig, while Ellen DeGeneres earns $224,000 per day or a cool $56 million per year hosting her daytime talk show. Authors of select literary projects might be very pleased to earn as much as $75,000,[12] but the success of Harry Potter has made author J. K. Rowling richer than the Queen of England.

So it goes for Artistic careers. Most of the people employed in creative and unconventional careers earn a decent but moderate salary, a small number are destitute, and an even smaller number become rich and famous. For every Bon Jovi or J. K. Rowling, there are thousands more aspiring to the top position, and they have no guarantees that they will ever be fairly rewarded.

I am not suggesting that all Artistic types are chasing fame and fortune. My guess is that most people, creative or more conventional, are happy to earn a decent living sharing their talents and doing work they enjoy. However, not being able to count on a steady salary is a scary prospect for anyone who needs job security or, perhaps more to the point, for those whose significant others want them to have security!

This may sound depressing. I'm simply trying to be objective here, not discouraging. Just because creative endeavors often lead to insecure employment doesn't mean you shouldn't pursue them. As you will learn, you can be a creative person in a conventional world and still have lots of viable work options and find creative success. And when you are successful, you can be really proud of what you have accomplished. After all, if it were easy, if there were no risks to take or dragons to slay, then it wouldn't be much of an accomplishment—or much of an adventure, either.

EMOTIONAL CONSEQUENCES OF A MISMATCH

If there are more Artistic people than there are jobs for them, then it follows that for every Artistic person doing Artistic work, there are kindred spirits who aren't. What are they doing? Usually, they are either underemployed or working in an environment in which they don't belong. Neither situation feels good and, if both are true, it's doubly distressing.

Let's look at underemployment first. Creative work requires a very high level of skill. In fact, the formal training and qualifications of the creative worker are higher than that of the general worker. It feels bad to have a high level of ability but not use it. One major study found that underutilization of abilities is positively related to job dissatisfaction, low self-esteem, and depression.[13] When people had more education than was required to perform their jobs, they experienced greater boredom, job dissatisfaction, physical complaints, and depression than people whose jobs fit their education.[14]

One of the best parts of having a job that fits your personality is the opportunity to work with birds of a feather. Just as it is agreeable to be with others who share your outlook on the world, it can feel awful to be an oddball. Media anthropologist Susan Allen says, "The notion that we should be like everyone else, even in this most individualistic of cultures, is immensely strong—and, among the fanatical of any persuasion, it is rigid. Kermit the Frog had it right when he sighed, 'It's not easy being green.'"[15]

It's not easy being an Artistic type employed on the wrong side of Holland's hexagon, either. Occasionally someone who is different is appreciated and valued for his or her uniqueness. More commonly, though, an Artistic type in a non-Artistic environment feels like the ugly duckling. Others see that person not as a swan out of place, but as a bad duck. When I worked as a waitress, I was surprised by how negatively my performance and even simply being at the restaurant affected my mood and self-esteem. My sense of self wasn't as independent of my job as I had thought it would be, and I lost confidence and began to wonder if I could be good at anything—in spite of a strong previous track record of success as a student!

> "A healthy, decent man never acts, paints, writes, or composes."
>
> —THOMAS MANN

Although I found the lack of respect I received from the restaurant staff unpleasant, it was nothing compared to the scapegoating that can happen when people are truly different. Being considered bad may be better than being completely ignored. As African-American writer Ralph Ellison pointed out in *Invisible Man*, the majority culture often denies that the minority individual exists at all. Among all human experiences, the invalidation that comes from not being seen, not being recognized, is among the most painful.

Perhaps the best way to sum up is to say that in the average work setting, the creative person does not fit in. Because psychological adjustment is defined, in part, as the ability to fit in, it's not too surprising to learn that Artistic types as a group demonstrate the least confidence and the greatest psychological distress of all six types. Again and again, the findings from psychological and vocational studies indicate that interests in art, music, and literature are associated with more psychological problems.

Among people with aesthetic interests, men are more likely than women to show signs of emotional distress. Some explanation may be found in the double standard our society has for artistic pursuits: it's okay for women but not for men—unless the man happens to be very successful. A male actor I knew once described with some bitterness how hard it was for him to admit he was an actor, because he experienced instant disrespect for not being a Tom Hanks or a Russell Crowe.

It's easy to speculate that the psychological health of creative people would improve if a good job fit were easier to achieve, and the data indicate that this is so. Although limited data pertain specifically to Artistic types, a good job-personality fit has been found in a number of studies to be positively related to self-esteem, mental health, and life satisfaction and negatively related to anxiety and burnout. College students whose majors match their Holland code show better personal adjustment than nonmatching students. Although causal links between job fit and mental health are not clear, one study of employees' mental health concluded: "Career and work satisfaction emerged as the strongest contributors to mental health."[16]

After all this discussion of the emotional consequences of being an unconventional person in a conventional work world, you might like to know how well your present job matches your personality. The questionnaire "Does Your Job Fit Your Personal Strengths?" can help you determine your current fit (see page 26). The more items you answer positively ("Yes," "Most," or "All"), the better fit you already have. The more items you answer negatively, the more you need to consider what you can do to find a better fit. The rest of this book can help you with that task.

What if your present occupation is not a good fit? Well, like most of us, you probably underestimate how much your job contributes to your sense of well-being. Perhaps I sound like a broken record here, but I think this truth is so important that it bears repeating: your work environment is likely to be more important than you think and to affect not only your feelings of happiness and self-worth but also your physical health and longevity! Yes, satisfaction with your job is associated with living a longer life.[17]

If you don't fit in at your current workplace, you can change it. Believe me, it will be a lot easier to change your job or employer than your personality. When you choose the environment you work in and the kind of work you do, it is worth choosing carefully, for it may be the single most important decision you ever make. Think about it: your work affects not only how you will spend sixty-five thousand hours of your adult life (if you are thirty), but also your happiness, your lifestyle, your sense of self, your circle of friends and inclusion in society, your opportunity to be rewarded for your talent, and your chance to make a meaningful contribution to the needs of our world.

Are you feeling discontented? I almost hope so, because feeling discontented can fuel you with the energy and motivation to set off on an adventure. Our adventure begins by looking inward. We'll shift focus now, from an objective, external survey of the world of work to the subjective, internal landscape of your creative personality.

DOES YOUR JOB FIT YOUR PERSONAL STRENGTHS?

FEW	SOME	MOST	ALL	
☐	☐	☐	☐	I like my coworkers.
☐	☐	☐	☐	I have good friends at work.
☐	☐	☐	☐	People I work with share my values.
☐	☐	☐	☐	People I work with respect my skills.

NO	SOMEWHAT	YES	
☐	☐	☐	My job utilizes my talents.
☐	☐	☐	My job draws upon my knowledge and education.
☐	☐	☐	My job is related to my interests.
☐	☐	☐	At work I get to work on problems I think are important.
☐	☐	☐	My work feels meaningful to me.
☐	☐	☐	I am proud of the role I play (who I get to be) at work.
☐	☐	☐	I am able to express myself at work.
☐	☐	☐	At work I am rewarded for my contribution, financially and/or through praise and positive recognition.

Chapter 2
THE CREATIVE PERSONALITY

In the last chapter, we learned that in the average work environment, creative people feel a mismatch. In this chapter we will look more closely at the ways in which creative people don't fit in, and I will try to help you see your own unique spin on being different. The better you understand your creative self, the better you will be able to attain an optimal fit. There is a paradox here, in that the traits that make you different are generally the same traits that make you best suited to a specific creative job. You can fit in if you find the right environment!

There is always the temptation to deny or hide our differences or to spend years trying to change parts of ourselves that we later conclude aren't changeable. I still sometimes resist saying what's on my mind, because I don't like being the one with the strange new ideas that make other people feel uncomfortable. When it comes to your career, though, I believe that the best approach is to understand and accept your differences, and then look for environments in which being the unique person you are is a terrific advantage.

So, what kind of person are you, anyway? We'll be focusing here on characteristics that describe the creative person, and a good way to start is to look at the traits typical of each Holland type. The personality traits listed below are grouped according to Holland's early research. Check those adjectives that you think best describe your personality, and then compare across groups once again to see which of the types you most closely resemble and which you least resemble.

ARTISTIC

- complicated
- disorderly
- emotional
- expressive
- idealistic
- imaginitive
- impractical
- impulsive
- independent
- introspective
- intuitive
- nonconforming
- open
- original
- sensitive

___Total Artistic Traits

SOCIAL

- ascendant
- cooperative
- friendly
- generous
- helpful
- idealistic
- kind
- patient
- persuasive
- responsible
- sociable
- tactful
- understanding
- warm

___Total Social Traits

ENTERPRISING

- acquisitive
- adventurous
- agreeable
- ambitious
- domineering
- energetic
- excitement-seeking
- exhibitionistic
- extroverted
- flirtatious
- optimistic
- self-confident
- sociable
- talkative

___Total Enterprising Traits

INVESTIGATIVE

- analytical
- cautious
- critical
- complex
- curious

- independent
- introspective
- intellectual
- pessimistic
- precise

- rational
- reserved
- retiring
- unassuming
- unpopular

___Total Investigative Traits

REALISTIC

- asocial
- conforming
- frank
- genuine
- hard-headed

- inflexible
- materialistic
- natural
- normal
- persistent

- practical
- self-effacing
- thrifty
- uninsightful
- uninvolved

___Total Realistic Traits

CONVENTIONAL

- careful
- conforming
- conscientious
- defensive
- efficient

- inflexible
- inhibited
- methodical
- obedient
- orderly

- persistent
- practical
- prudish
- thrifty
- unimaginitive

___Total Conventional Traits

The adjectives you checked will probably appear in many of the six categories, rather than just one. This is to be expected, because each Holland type is an abstract theoretical model that perfectly describes no real person like you. You may find that some of the Artistic adjectives don't apply in your case, but that doesn't mean that you are not creative. Among people who I think are highly creative, I've met some who tell me their creativity is the only thing they feel confident about and others who say they don't even believe they are creative! If you feel doubtful about your creativity, try to be open to discovering new aspects of yourself.

In scientific creativity, in the Investigative corner of Holland's hexagon, the problems tend to be about physical reality, and the solutions are mostly the result of brainwork. It's a more objective form of creativity. In Artistic creativity, on the other hand, you start with something out there, but then you take it inside. It's a more subjective, emotional form of creativity. It's brainwork, but also soul work. Your psyche becomes intimately involved and grows and changes as part of the creative process.

> "At its basic level the creative process is simply the solving of problems that stand in the way of attaining a dream."
>
> —HARRY DENT JR.

Have you ever noticed that in the best adventure stories, heroes have not only an external problem to solve, but an internal one as well? Their task is not simply to improve life for the greater social good, but also to overcome a personal vulnerability. The two challenges, outer and inner, are set up in parallel, so that the heroes' personal struggles become a juicy part of the story. In short, the creative process carries with it an internal journey.

Before you embark on your own creative career adventure, you might appreciate a preview. Here's my quick summary of that process: First, creative people are sensitive to some aspect of reality. As they perceive that part of reality, stimulated by both good and bad feelings, they find problems. They work with those problems, thinking, learning, experimenting, and developing new skills. Eventually, they produce new and better solutions.

That description sounds rather serious, as though all problems that inspire the creative process are heavy and significant, and all effort is conscious and deliberate. But the survival of the entire world doesn't hang in the balance in every adventure! Troubles can also be of a lighter and more playful sort. Maybe your difficulty is that you don't like your first watercolor efforts—so you take a painting class. Or you're tired of birdhouses that all look the same, and new designs come to you spontaneously. Whatever problem you tackle, the creative process is similar.

> "An artist is not a special kind of person. Every person is a special kind of artist."
>
> —**MEISTER ECKHART**

> "A work of art is a corner of creation seen through a temperament."
>
> —**ÉMILE ZOLA**

Now we will look at the creative personality in greater depth, proceeding from the perceptions of creative people to their feelings and thoughts and finally to their behavior. As we shall see, creative people tend to be sensitive to their perceptions, intuitive in their problem-solving, expressive of their feelings, divergent in their thinking, and independent in their behavior.

SENSITIVITY TO PERCEPTIONS

Creativity begins with perception. Perception means both taking in sensory information (seeing, hearing, tasting, touching, or smelling) and giving meaning to that information in the mind. Maybe you sniff something and recognize the scent as floral or herbal. Or you touch fibers and know from their warmth and resilience that they are wool. The act of reading this book is a visual perceptual experience—your eyes pick up little black shapes on a white page, but your mind recognizes the forms of letters and gives meaning to words.

The Greek word *aisthanesthai*, "to perceive," is the root of the word *aesthetics*. Artistic types value aesthetics. They are likely to value beauty as much as an Enterprising type would value making a profit or a Conventional type would value keeping the record straight. Although the Realistic, Conventional, and Enterprising types might appreciate their art objects more for the status of ownership or for their financial value, Artistic types would be more likely to value works of art for their aesthetic qualities. Or they might appreciate something beautiful without wanting to own it at all.

Sensitivity to beauty may paradoxically bring pain as well as pleasure. A calligrapher friend of mine once told me that she was pained by the ugly and ordinary lettering of storefront signs in her neighborhood. Similarly, after refining my appreciation of literature in college, I suffered both as an English teacher and as a psychology student when I was required to read poorly written prose. It is like being a wine connoisseur confronted with a glass of fermented grape juice. An artistic sensitivity to something combines the potential for a sublime experience with the agony of confrontation with the ordinary.

Creative people appear to be more sensitive than others. A psychological researcher found that, compared to people who were less creative, creative people were more reactive to perceptual experience—they overestimated the intensity of electric shock and overestimated the size of wood they touched but couldn't see, and their brain waves were upset for a longer period of time in response to a high-pitched sound. He concluded that the brains of creative types operated at a higher level of arousal and that "creative people view the world and react to it unlike most of their peers, not because they are eccentric and strange, but because they process information differently."[18]

As part of processing information differently, creative people tend to be open and receptive, better able to dwell in their senses, without preconceptions. Artist Georgia O'Keeffe commented on her perceptual experience with a flower—taking time to really look instead of hurrying by with no more than a glance:

"A flower is relatively small. Everyone has many associations with a flower—the idea of flowers. You put out your hand to touch the flower— lean forward to smell it—maybe touch it with your lips almost without thinking—or give it to someone to please them. Still—in a way—nobody sees a flower—really—it is so small—we haven't time—and to see takes time like to have a friend takes time. If I could paint the flower exactly as I see it no one would see what I see because I would paint it small like the flower is small.

"So I said to myself—I'll paint what I see—what the flower is to me but I'll paint it big and they will be surprised into taking time to look at it."[19]

O'Keeffe is like other artists in her visual sensitivity. Many creative people are unusually sensitive to some aspect of their everyday sensory experience. For example, some people notice and remember sound, which makes them more likely to become interested in music. Musicians hear more: their ears detect more subtle distinctions, picking up timbre, overtones, harmonies, and counterpoint, whereas less-sensitive listeners may hear only a sound or a single melody. Dancers respond to movement. Writers are attuned to language. Dramatists keenly observe human behavior.[20]

Sensitivity varies both within and across individuals. We can be very sensitive to some perceptual experiences but less sensitive to others. For example, my husband is more sensitive to taste than I am: he experiences a cup of coffee and a cinnamon roll with a pleasure that I envy. I am more sensitive to language and emotion than he is, and I enjoy novels and movies with more discernment than he does.

However, my sensitivity to language doesn't mean that I pick up all information equally well. In fact, I'm not so observant when it comes to moving through space. Anybody who has ever watched me parallel park would have to conclude that I have a pretty dim idea of where the curb is relative to the car! And I'm not alone in that regard: people who are quite perceptive about one domain may miss a lot of information in others.

In recognizing my own creativity, it has helped to focus on those areas in which I am most sensitive. For example, I have more word sense than muscle sense, and I am a better writer than I am a dancer. I am more sensitive to personality than I am to music, and I am better at recognizing psychological differences among people than I am at recognizing tones in music. That's typical. Most of us are not uniform in our talents: our creativity is most evident in a few domains.

How about you? To what are you most sensitive? There are so many different possibilities: space, light, sound, fragrance, textiles, landscape, and on and on. You could also be sensitive to less tangible, more human phenomena, such as character, community, or social justice. Think about your own areas of sensitivity and how they differ from those of other people you know. If you are not sure what kinds of perceptual experiences give you the greatest pleasure, flip the question around and think about the kinds of ugliness that most distress you.

Let me illustrate how your unique sensitivity could relate to your career. One of my clients was exquisitely sensitive to color, and she used this talent on the job. She was a costume designer who could make one hundred costumes come out the identical shade of blue, because she knew by gazing into dye lots exactly how many drops of dye were needed to make a perfect match. And when the art director came to her and said that he wanted a costume "the color of the earth, rich and warm and fecund," she was able to go from his words to a color that sent him into rapture.

Or consider a better-known example. Cartoonist Scott Adams was sensitive to absurdity and had the opportunity to behold plenty of it when he worked in an American corporation. He mined that sensitivity to the delight of millions of readers of his *Dilbert* comic strip. Adams's sensitivity called his attention to morale problems created by workplace bureaucracy, office politics, and incompetent management.

Researchers of creativity have given as much attention to problems as to solutions. Problem-finding is thought to be at least as important to creativity as problem-solving. "The creative process," wrote psychologist Donald MacKinnon, "starts always with the seeing or sensing of a problem. The roots of creativeness lie in one's becoming aware that something is wrong, or lacking, or mysterious. One of the salient traits of a truly creative person is that he sees problems where others don't . . ."[21]

What kind of problems are we talking about? All kinds. Take your pick. It could be a personal difficulty, like how best to express yourself. Or an artistic or spiritual puzzle, like how to reveal the mysterious. Or you might be motivated by more practical or global dilemmas, like how to foster world peace or how to protect the environment. There is no shortage of challenges. Whether your problems are small or large, personal or universal, already defined or still unformulated, the creative search for solutions can be joyous and deeply engaging.

> "It is said that a question well posed is half-answered. If so, then true invention consists in the posing of questions. There is something mechanical, as it were, in the art of finding solutions. The truly original mind is that which finds problems."
>
> **—PAUL SOURIAU**

INTUITIVE PROBLEM-SOLVING

Intuition is an unconscious perceptual process that picks up on potential problems and possible solutions. The mysterious process of intuition is a way to "see beyond" the reality presented to your senses. According to the psychologist Carl Jung, sensation is a perceptive process that focuses on actuality—the facts—whereas intuition is a process that focuses on possibility—the relationships among the facts. It's the difference between what is and what could be, between reality as it is commonly accepted and the discovery of previously unrecognized connections.

Sensory thinking is usually linear: A leads to B leads to C. Intuitive thinking, on the other hand, is more likely to occur in leaps, leaving you as an intuitive thinker unsure of how you reached your conclusion: A leads to C, and you are not aware of bypassing B. Often this is experienced as the excitement of a creative insight: the "Eureka!" experience.

Think, for example, of Archimedes, who had been struggling for a way to measure volume. It is unlikely that when he sat down in the bathtub he thought, "My body in the tub is like any body in water; the rise of the water is a way of measuring the volume taken up by any object; I have found a way to measure volume." It is more likely that his "Eureka!" preceded his step-by-step analysis.

We all use both sensation and intuition as ways of picking up information from the world around us. However, each of us tends to prefer one mode over the other, to achieve greater strength in the preferred mode, and to engage in it more often. Although there are always exceptions, Artistic types show a strong preference for intuition. Opposite them on the hexagon, Conventional types show a strong preference for sensation. As far as career choice is concerned, a more practical way to say this is that Artistic work revolves around ideas, whereas Conventional work revolves around data.

> "Of our conflicts with others we make rhetoric; of our conflicts with ourselves we make poetry."
>
> **—WILLIAM BUTLER YEATS**

Creative and unconventional people are more likely to focus on the big picture than on the details—unless, of course, they are focusing on the details regarding their areas of special interest. There they often find problems and come up with solutions that others don't. To the more forthright and practical sensing person, the creative person's intuitions may seem flaky or off-the-wall. Some strongly intuitive creative people may occasionally feel misunderstood and unfairly judged as lacking in intellectual ability by their more linear and left-brained colleagues.

Whether left-brained or right-brained, sensing or intuiting, everyone feels and thinks about what she or he has perceived. Feeling and thinking are presented in the following sections as though they are distinct and sequential but, of course, they interact in a more complex fashion.

EXPRESSIVE OF FEELINGS

Artistic types describe themselves as emotional and expressive, which fits the stereotype of the moody and temperamental artist. Although some of their emotion is positive, such as the romantic love celebrated in popular music, much of it is not. In fact, negative emotionality is related to creativity. This may surprise you because creativity is so often confused with social desirability. After reading many psychological studies of creative people, however, I am struck by how often they are described as possessing traits that are considered socially undesirable.

What traits have been used to describe creative and artistic people in psychological studies? Hostile, aggressive, dominant, and self-centered. Histrionic, rebellious, anxious, insecure, inconsiderate, irresponsible, and emotionally unstable. Yikes! If you feel offended, please note that these adjectives reflect the biases of the researchers and a certain amount of immaturity in the subjects. For a look at more mature creativity, see the last chapter in this book.

Please be assured that poor mental health is not required to do creative work. Far from it. Also, it may be the case that symbolic work by its very nature becomes something of a double-edged sword. According to the developers of Acceptance and Commitment Therapy (ACT), problem-solving efforts with words, numbers, images—absolutely any kind of symbol system—brings with it a greater vulnerability to mental and emotional pain, engendering a problem-solving attitude that doesn't know when to call it quits.[22]

The intuitive preference for what could be, rather than what is, helps produce some negative feelings. Creative people often focus on what is wrong, what is missing, what needs to be changed to make something better. In fact, many creative people look like chronic malcontents to outsiders, because they are always searching for what can be improved. On the Strong Interest Inventory assessment, a test commonly used to help students choose careers, the Artistic type checks "dislike" in answer to the test questions more frequently than any other type!

Conflict is a word often encountered in psychological explanations of creativity. The very richness and complexity associated with conflict yields a more creative product. The sensitive Artistic person perceives a complex world in which certain elements are wrong or don't fit—and then experiences internal conflict as part of the creative process of refitting them. The conflict comes, in part, because the Artistic person does not rest content with old forms.

> "Medicine, to produce health, has to examine disease; and music, to create harmony, must investigate discord."
>
> **—PLUTARCH**

Such internal conflict may help produce the emotional states that others perceive as moodiness and histrionics. Perhaps it can even help account for the fact that creators seem to suffer disproportionately from mood disorders such as depression.

Critical, challenging, independent, risk-taking—these are characteristics of many creative people. If you are an agent of change, if you question and challenge the status quo, if you express your pain and protest, then you are likely to be seen as a troublemaker and to make others feel uncomfortable. Although it is certainly the case that many creative and unconventional people present their sweet, gentle, agreeable aspects to the world and control or hide their destructive impulses, it is important to realize that creativity has its negative consequences.

Surely other people are also dissatisfied and emotional. They are human beings living in the same imperfect world. But conventional people more frequently suppress or repress the feelings that artistically creative people express. A psychological understanding of how you deal with anxiety may be helpful here. Although being closed and seeing the world in simple and concrete terms may better enable you to manage your anxiety, admitting to yourself a more complex worldview may lead to greater anxiety—as well as greater creativity. Many psychological studies have found that creative people are both more anxious and less repressed than "normals." They don't deny that things trouble them.

Although artistically creative people are often impulsive and dramatic, they may have difficulty communicating their feelings directly. I remember watching one of my artistic roommates create a work of art for a boyfriend with whom she had fought. Rather than going to him and saying, "I love you and I am sad that I hurt you," she painted him a lovely picture that expressed those feelings. This is what Freud meant when he described the various art forms as sublimation—one of the most mature of the psychological strategies for dealing with anxiety. Sublimation may be understood as an unconscious means of expressing emotion through the distance of art.

> "Every act of creation is first of all an act of destruction."
>
> —**PABLO PICASSO**

David Copperfield, the magician, described it this way in an interview with the *Seattle Times*: "I started doing magic at ten and I had a lot of early success and approval. Magic became something I could do on stage and get paid for. I admired songwriters who could take elements of their lives and express themselves on stage. I try to do the same thing with magic. It's a way to communicate and to express myself." Not only magic but all art seems to be motivated by that basic urge: to express the Self. Artists want to communicate not just ideas but also the feelings that accompany them, and to do it in a way that will capture the attention and imagination of their audience.

To recognize your own unique spin on creativity, think about how you express yourself. Through which forms are your feelings most apparent and accessible to others? Images? Gestures? Language? Rhythm? It may be obvious, as it is with mimes like Marcel Marceau, whose performance is infused with emotion. But in some creative fields, feeling is expressed in less obvious ways. Industrial designers, for example, design cars that embody security or excitement and computers that make users feel more comfortable with technology.

DIVERGENT THINKING

Once creative people have found problems, they think about them. They use their intelligence, including a part of intelligence called convergent thinking. Convergent thinking is the ability to find the single right answer to a given problem. For example, you use convergent thinking to answer the following question: what is 2 + 2?

But in addition, creators typically employ a unique kind of thinking not related to intelligence called divergent thinking. Divergent thinking has to do with a rapid flow of ideas and the ability to come up with many possible solutions to a problem for which there is no single, correct, and already established answer. With divergent thinking, the brain's idea meter is naturally set on High. Creativity researchers call this "fluency." The Johnson O'Connor Research Foundation, an organization that tests human aptitudes, calls it "ideaphoria." Divergent thinking, like intuition, is considered an important aspect of creativity.

A visual example of a question from a divergent thinking test is shown on the following page.

If you were taking the test, you would be asked to include the given line in your own drawing of something that no one else would think of and to "keep adding new ideas to your first idea" until you had developed a picture that told an interesting story. A verbal example of a question on a divergent thinking test might be something like: "What would happen if all the water in the world were suddenly to freeze?" or "How many different ways can you use a brick?"

Divergent thinkers would be able to come up with many more responses to these kinds of questions than convergent thinkers. In addition, their answers would tend to be more variable, so that each reply didn't simply restate the same idea in a slightly different way. A few of their answers might even be quite unusual.

Divergent ideas may be plentiful but not particularly appropriate. For example, one of my creative friends had countless ideas for my career that I found unappealing, such as caring for orangutans in New Guinea, mass-marketing trout from my remote mountain cabin, and interviewing customers on video to help them create their own video diaries. Divergent thinkers sometimes look a little crazy and their ideas a little far-fetched to their convergent friends, because it is likely that many of their ideas won't work. But this is all part of the creative process. After all, at one time it was absurd to think

> "Civilization is a slow process of adopting the ideas of minorities."
>
> —HERBERT PROCHNOW

the world might be round. We tend to forget that the few ideas that are socially valued evolved out of a process in which many less appropriate ideas were abandoned.

The divergent thinker's ability to come up with a great many ideas increases the likelihood that at least one of the new ideas will work. That is the essence of creativity: a new idea that works. A creative idea needs to be both (1) new or original or novel and (2) adaptive or appropriate or functional. Sometimes creative ideas are also either generative (they inspire new, related ideas) or influential (they change their domain). Obviously, the thinking that produces such effective ideas can't be entirely divergent. Although divergent thinking helps you produce many possibilities, convergent thinking helps you choose the one best solution to the problem.

> "A good idea has, as it were, self-expanding qualities. It stimulates those who see it to add to it."
>
> —JAMES WEBB YOUNG

Although I sound very appreciative of divergent thinking, you should know that I yelped when my editor bombarded me with lots of ideas for changing the first edition of this book. When I expressed my dismay over new ideas not in line with my vision, she said, "My mind tends to leap ahead of the immediate problem, create more problems, and come up with possibilities no one needs or wants. Fortunately, an occasional good one creeps in there, too." Many creative people might describe their cognitive style in a similar way.

INDEPENDENT BEHAVIOR

All those different ideas lead to some different behavior. What can creators discover that will effectively solve their problem? They experiment to find out: the Wright brothers experimented with kites and gliders and flyers before they invented the world's first airplane; Mahatma Gandhi experimented with different forms of social protest before he perfected his process for nonviolent noncompliance; Martha Graham experimented with dance steps and breathing techniques in the process of developing modern dance.

Although the Wrights and Gandhi and Graham behaved very differently from each other, these highly creative people were alike in that they each marched to their own drummer. And in that sense, they resemble creative and unconventional people everywhere. When you stick with the status quo, you've got lots of company; if you do something new, then you go your own way. So it is fortunate that Artistic types tend to be independent and self-sufficient.

One researcher concluded, "A protest against a great deal of parental concern, the desire to be free and untrammeled, to resist superimposed structure and standards, to be nonconformist . . . can be inferred from high artistic interest . . ."[23] Not surprisingly, of the six Holland types, the Artistic type is the least influenced by social factors such as what their family, friends, and teachers think. Their career choices are more influenced by what they like and are drawn to, often causing family concern that they don't know what they are doing or what is best for them.

> "Individuality of expression is the beginning and end of all art."
>
> **—JOHANN WOLFGANG VON GOETHE**

> "Art is the most intense mode of individualism that the world has known."
>
> **—OSCAR WILDE**

Although some creative people are so unconventional that they avoid school completely, many Artistic types are well educated. This is a group that aspires to and achieves a high level of academic status: master's degrees and doctorates are not uncommon. It has been found that the longer a person engages in formal education, in fact, the more her or his interest in aesthetics increases. A formal liberal

> "Divergers are less interested in success, more interested in self-expression. They chose unusual occupations, such as inventor or entertainer, rather than the more conventional doctor or lawyer."
>
> —LEONA TYLER

arts education was designed to train people to think for themselves, freeing them from convention so they might choose their own paths.

Artistic types tend to avoid business and practical courses of study, seeking out the theoretical and abstract. They major in the fine arts, liberal arts, or humanities. Investigative types, on the other hand, are likely to major in science or engineering; Realistic types, in agriculture (or they may get vocational training or join the military). Social types are likely to end up in colleges of education or social work; Enterprising and Conventional types, in business.

Although the other Holland types pursue degrees that translate readily into actual jobs, Artistic people are likely to take courses that do not lead directly to employment, and they may spend extracurricular time in such activities as dance, debate, comedy, photography, or school publications. This academic path is likely to be seen by others as idealistic and impractical. After all, what does one do with a degree in women's studies or Eastern philosophy?

A high Artistic score on a vocational interest test may be said to reflect an appreciation for the finer things in life. Although the stereotype of the artist is a creator, very often the Artistic person is an appreciator rather than a creator. In this sense, too, your educational endeavors may be seen as impractical. If it is hard to make your living by creating, it is doubly hard to make your living by appreciating. As I know from personal experience, you can spend many years and thousands of tuition dollars learning to appreciate the great achievements of Western civilization—only to find yourself washing dishes or waiting tables!

Creative people tend to be nonconforming in their relation to authority figures. They want to do their own thing their own way. The first time I led a career group for creative and unconventional people, I was struck by the number of group members who described conflict with their bosses as part of their work woes. If you are independent, the worst kind of boss is the kind who breathes down your neck and micromanages your efforts. Creative people are happier at work, better able get into an innovative flow state, if they are given enough freedom to make their own decisions. They value autonomy.

Seen from this perspective, it makes sense that Artistic types would avoid Conventional work, which is in part defined as adhering to a given structure, maintaining the established order, or following explicit directions to accomplish an explicit task. For tasks such as filing, typing, and accounting, which are Conventional in nature, it makes great sense that the worker does the work the way it has always been done. If you are Artistic, though, these kinds of routine clerical duties feel like death to the soul. Not only have you lost your freedom in the 9-to-5 grind, but you have also lost all personal freedom in doing the work itself.

A sensitive, intuitive, expressive nature is no advantage when the task is to handle everyday maintenance chores by established rules. In fact, you may find that you are less efficient and more tired out by the work than other people would be. Because so many of the jobs that are readily available are conventional jobs, you may get down on yourself and think, "I just don't like to work." You may not realize that it's that particular kind of work that's so distasteful to you, not all work.

Creative people do like to work at tasks for which they feel intrinsic motivation. Consider the following quote from *The Creative Vision,* a study of young art students at the Art Institute of Chicago:

> *"The four major reasons the artists gave for painting or sculpting— discovery in general, self-knowledge, understanding other people, and the quest for reality—are, of course, closely interrelated. Taken together, they seem to point to a deep existential commitment to coming to terms*

with life. If we are to trust the self-report of artists, this, and not the usual external rewards of a profession, is what motivates them to devote their lives to their vocation."[24]

The usual external rewards of a profession—money, status, and power, for example—motivate the Enterprising, Conventional, and Realistic types more than they do the Artistic type. Of course, Artistic people would like to make lots of money and indulge in some luxuries and be treated with deference and respect, but their strongest ambitions are more subtle. It is the opportunity to do the work itself that motivates, especially given the by-products of discovery and personal understanding. They value creative activity for its own sake.

Steven Soderbergh described that kind of personal motivation for writing the script of *Sex, Lies, and Videotape*. In an interview with the *Seattle Times*, he explained that he wrote the screenplay following his breakup with someone very important to him, and that he was obsessed with what he had done to cause the breakup. He wanted to understand what had happened and how he could prevent it from happening in the future.

"A genius is a person who, seeing farther and probing deeper than other people, has a different set of ethical valuations from theirs, and has energy enough to give effect to this extra vision and its valuations in whatever manner best suits his or her specific talents."

—GEORGE BERNARD SHAW

Perhaps the most apt general descriptive statement about Artistic people is that they prefer unstructured work environments with opportunities for self-expression. The fine arts provide the least structure and the greatest opportunity to express the self. However, creativity is certainly not limited to the fine arts. Applied fields such as journalism and advertising and interior design are also relatively unstructured and expressive. In addition, there are other kinds of creative opportunities. An Enterprising person, for example, could bring new businesses into existence. An entrepreneurial start-up can provide freedom to innovate along with the potential of great financial rewards.

HOW TO MAKE THIS WORK FOR YOU

We have come to the end of our tour of the creative personality, and I hope you have gained a better understanding of what's going on inside yourself. Did a number of those creative characteristics describe you? Are you sensitive and expressive? Intuitive and independent? Do you value beauty and autonomy? Do you have lots of ideas? Do you like to experiment with different ways of doing things?

If so, you might ask those who don't understand you to read this chapter, and maybe they'll become more tolerant once they realize that it's legitimate for you to be different from them. More important, I hope that if you have been critical of your creative temperament in the past, you will become more accepting and appreciative of yourself in the future. It is okay to be the way you are. It's okay to study the arts. Even better than that—it's valuable.

In my case, it took me some time to appreciate the value of my English major. At first, it seemed to me that I'd chosen a path that led to no job I wanted, and I beat myself up for being so impractical. Later, I realized more of the true worth that accompanied my love of literature. For example, the literary arts showed me how passion and artistry add value to ideas that might otherwise seem dry and uninteresting. Reading literature also developed my abilities to imagine the lives of others and empathize with them, which I was later able to utilize as a counselor and writer.

> "Above all, don't improve yourself. Improve the world, so that your characteristics stop being problems."
>
> —BARBARA SHER

It will be the rare person who reads this chapter and finds that everything describes him or her perfectly. Any theory that categorizes people, including Holland's, can be too stereotyped. Some parts of my description of the creative personality most likely won't be true for you, and that is as it should be. Artistic types usually don't want so much to be like other Artistic types as they want to be unlike all types. In fact, what they may really want is to be recognized for how they are individual, truly different, and the exceptional exception.

That being the case, how can you make the ideas in this chapter work for you? How can you take maximum advantage of the ways in which you are different, not only from the average person but also from the average creative person? My recommendation is to identify the different parts of yourself that combine to make you unique. Although you can almost always find someone who has more of characteristic X than you do, your uniqueness lies not in having more X, but in having those other attributes that you can combine with X.

Let me illustrate what I mean. A great entrepreneur has more than a new business idea; he or she can also apply that idea in a profitable way. A great basketball player has more than height; he or she also possesses athletic ability and a competitive spirit. A great model needs more than a well-proportioned and slender body; he or she also benefits from attractive features, a clear complexion, perfect posture, and poise.

Success in any given domain depends on more than active interest or native talent or any other single characteristic. Success comes from a combination of qualities. New Zealand photographer Anne Geddes provides an example. Geddes combines her sensitivity to images with an interest in babies. She creates simple, emotional images with wide appeal: her photography books have sold millions of copies in scores of countries. Her success wasn't just that she could photograph, but that she chose a subject she loved, continued to experiment with her camera technique, and also applied her business skills.

So it is with your career. You start with a subject or field that attracts you. What you do next depends on the other qualities that are also a part of you. Although those other qualities might be present in thousands of people on this planet (lots of people are photographers and lots of people love babies), their combination in you will be unique (just as they were for Anne Geddes). It is a unique package that you offer to an employer, whether that employer is a corporation, a company, or an individual client.

Although I don't think of myself as an employer, I had similar concerns when I sought a co-author to help me refresh this edition. I needed someone who: 1) was currently active as a career counselor, 2) was able to write well, 3) felt genuine enthusiasm for the project, and 4) would act in a friendly and trustworthy manner. I was very fortunate to find Carrie Pinsky, who possesses all those qualities and more. In fact, she was already using the third edition of this career guide to assist liberal arts students at our local university. It turns out Carrie's Holland code is ASE—Artistic, Social, and Enterprising. She admits spending much of her career denying and downplaying her creative aspirations because they seemed impractical and separate from her professional goals. When she described herself as earlier in her life "waiting for a knight on a white charger to come save her" from her career troubles, I knew I'd found my co-author!

The rest of this book will help you combine your abilities and values with your interests. In fact, I've developed a set of online tools you can use to identify your interests, abilities, and values. My support tools were developed when I worked with career clients in person and online. They are now part of a framework for creating a personalized notebook dedicated to career choice and job search. You'll find more information about the notebook in chapter 5.

In the next section, we will focus less on Holland's theory and interests and more on creative abilities and how they can direct you through our often-bewildering world of work.

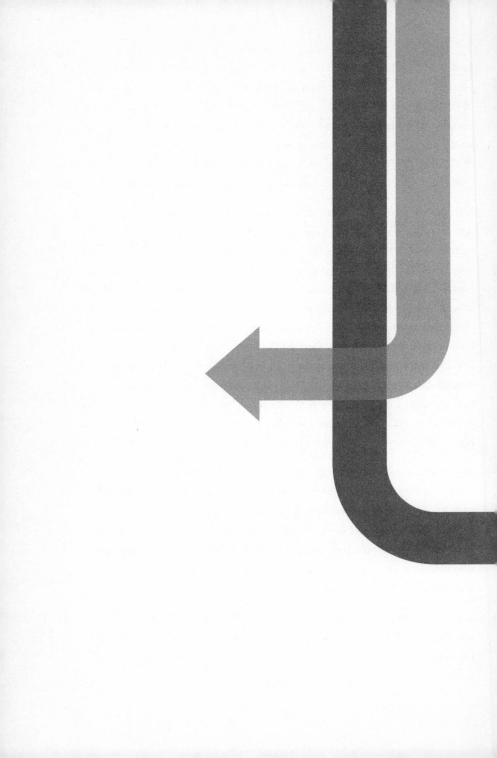

PART TWO

POSSIBLE SOLUTIONS

"In choosing an occupation one is, in effect, choosing a means of implementing a self-concept."
—DONALD SUPER

"Dwell in possibility."
—EMILY DICKINSON

Chapter 3
CREATIVE CAREER CHOICES

Having learned about what's going on, both outside in the world of work and inside your creative personality, it's time to set off on a personal quest to find your ideal career. Here we will look at the work opportunities that best match the person you are. If you already know what you want to do, you can skip this chapter. But even if you are already pretty well matched with your current job or course of study, you might like to explore in a new direction. One simple truth prevails: You have options. Options are liberating and especially helpful to anyone who feels trapped or stuck.

This middle part of this book provides you with an abundance of career choices. In this chapter, you'll find twenty-five different categories that lead to the 281 different occupations in the Career Reference Section at the back of the book. Each occupational entry includes a variety of employers. In the next chapter, you'll find eight different ways to arrange work in a creative lifestyle, along with a variety of social media to support your arrangement.

Of course, when you are presented with lots of options, you eventually need to choose from among them, and that presents its own hazards. In fact, making decisions feels risky to many people, and in their haste to get it done and behind them, they sometimes shortchange the process via two common pitfalls: first, they don't consider enough options; second, they don't get enough information about the options under consideration. I will help you now to discover a number of options; later, you'll receive guidance regarding how to get more information on the options that are the most attractive to you. Then you can weigh the pros and cons and trust your intuition to help you make a good choice.

YOUR SKILLS

Assuming you already know that you have artistic interests and a creative personality, the most important self-knowledge you need to acquire now is knowledge about your abilities. As we saw in the first part of the book, aesthetic interests alone don't lead to employment. When I help clients choose a career, I usually spend as much time on their abilities as I do on their vocational interests. Interests and abilities together point to an occupation.

Abilities are an innate capacity to learn to do something quickly and well. In this regard we all vary. Someone who is talented has a high ability compared to others in one particular area, such as eye-hand coordination or numerical reasoning or flow of ideas. In this chapter we'll consider what your special talents might be.

In adventure stories, villains often attack heroes—but heroes possess a unique advantage, because they are born with an affinity for a particular ability, such as using a sword. And part of the hero's journey is to develop their talent and, through practice and training, build their swordplay skills, which later save the day.

In like manner, you need to discover your talents and train your strongest abilities, building a set of problem-solving skills that provide you with competitive advantage. You need to discover your greatest talents—those unique areas where you learn fastest and perform best—and then look for a career that requires your best abilities and does not reveal your weaknesses. You do not need to be good at everything.

Remember: Employers hire you for what you can do—especially when it's something that not everyone can do. Today's workers with ho-hum, everybody's-got-them skills can expect to languish. It's now more important than ever to possess a complex, conceptual skill set. Believe it or not, there is a growing skills shortage, so acute that competition for talent has gone global. That's right: Despite high unemployment, there are also a great number of jobs going unfilled. Companies need your talent so that they can compete on the world stage. However, it's up to you to show employers that you possess the skills they need.

More than any other factor, your skills help you translate who you are into a job. Skills are what you do, expressed as verbs (like modeling, writing, calculating, teaching, directing, and so on). Skills are what you do at work, and they can be used in any number of different jobs or hobbies. Your most important skills come from talents or aptitudes that you have developed over time. It feels good to use these skills; it may even feel bad not to use them. Knowing and using your native abilities lies at the heart of career development, as the following story illustrates.

Once a fifty-year-old woman who was not happy with her job came to see me for career counseling. I asked her how she saw the problem. The problem, she said, was that she was too young to retire. She was tired of working and ready to retire, but she couldn't afford to. Since she had to work, she wanted whatever she did to be as stress-free as possible. For her this meant no after-hours work. She wanted to leave the job behind at the end of an eight-hour workday to make maximum time for herself.

I asked her to do a skills analysis exercise and recommended the one in the book, *What Color Is Your Parachute?*[25] She did the exercise at home, and when she returned to see me for her next appointment, she was a different person. Now that she was more aware of her skills, she saw the problem differently. She said the problem was that her present job as a computer programmer processing office data didn't require her preferred skills. Through the skills analysis, she had learned her strength lay in communicating visual information. She had already targeted a new career that would allow her to use these skills: using the computer to design graphics so that she could depict information visually. Now that she had identified her true calling, she was excited. It was all right with her if she worked fourteen-hour days, because the work wouldn't feel stressful.

Her story is not unusual. When your work requires skills you already possess, you feel less stress. Your dependable strengths, as pioneering career counselor Bernard Haldane called them, come naturally to you. Your talents feel easy to use, because you don't have to force yourself or exert great amounts of discipline or willpower. In fact, your strengths are so close to your essence that it may feel almost impossible not to use them. When you work with your natural strengths, you usually enjoy the process and feel you're doing it well. It's like flying with the wind, instead of against it.

Besides helping you identify less-stressful ways to make a living, there are other advantages to knowing your abilities. One of them is that focusing on your abilities enhances self-esteem. Whether you call them skills, aptitudes, motivated abilities, dependable strengths, talents, or gifts, they are positive things about you. When you use them, you feel good about yourself. When you see that they are part of who you are and that they have been evident since your childhood, your confidence grows. You'll develop inner security about your ability to support yourself and to make a meaningful contribution by doing work that feels good and natural to you.

There are practical advantages, too. When you are aware of your strengths, you can be more articulate during your job hunt. Employers want to know about your abilities. Put your skills on your resume and talk about them in your job interview. When the interviewer says, "Tell me about yourself," describe your achievements. Say, "I can because I have. I can do this job because I have already done work like this, using skills X, Y, and Z." And then support your statements with concrete, relevant, detailed stories of accomplishments from your past.

In short, knowing your strengths will give you direction, decrease your stress, improve your self-esteem, and help you sell yourself to employers. However, many people remain ignorant of their true talents. Sadly enough, research confirms that most of us are not very good at estimating our own abilities. We're just too close to see ourselves objectively, so we need outside help.

How can you acquire this valuable self-knowledge? Let me suggest several ways. First of all, you might consider getting an objective test of your aptitudes. In the United States, I recommend private aptitude testing at the Johnson O'Connor Research Foundation, which is located in eleven major cities, and at Career Vision in the Chicago area. Career Vision also offers the Ball Aptitude Battery as an online assessment with a virtual meeting to share results.

Private aptitude testing is the most expensive option. Not everyone can afford it. However, you should know that a growing number of employers are screening a job candidate's aptitudes before hiring. In other words, job candidates get tested after they have already invested their time and money in training for a career. The cost of aptitude assessment is a tiny fraction of the cost of a college education, which is one reason I took the path of private testing for my own family.

A public assessment option that measures far fewer aptitudes, but is free in the United States, is the O*NET Ability Profiler (see www.onetcenter.org/AP.html). If you'd like to take this test, try contacting your local Career Workforce Center or CareerOneStop Center. The tests offered may vary by state and some options may even have different names. They are listed in the phone book under state or county government. A few high schools offer the Ability Profiler through their online career services.

Objective ability tests like those above are not always perfect, however. If your test results are inconsistent with other feedback you have received, like grades and praise, or if your test results seem to say that you can't do something you really want to do, then you will probably be better off sticking with self-estimates. Whatever your approach, the goal is to know yourself better so that you can pursue what you want to do in the manner most likely to succeed.

A good self-estimate option is the skills analysis in *What Color Is Your Parachute?* (also sold separately in a smaller, less expensive booklet, the *What Color Is Your Parachute? Job-Hunter's Workbook*[26]). An alternative to that skills analysis is provided in the book, *The Truth about You.*[27] In addition to helping you recognize your favorite skills, *The Truth about You* can help you discover the kinds of problems and rewards that truly motivate you. If you have trouble locating *The Truth about You*, try using the interlibrary loan service of your public library to obtain a copy.

Both the skills analysis in *Parachute* and the *Parachute Job-Hunter's Workbook* and the System for Identifying Motivated Abilities in *The Truth about You* ask you to look for patterns in your past activities. Strengths tend to show up at an early age and continue throughout your life. Because they have been with you a long time, they create patterns you can see once you know how to look for them.

A less laborious way to get a handle on your skills is to use a list of verbs. You can find such lists in many job-hunting books. My own list follows. I recommend that you go through this list twice. First, read through the list and underline those skills that you know you have and enjoy using. Then, go back through the underlined words and put a star next to those skills that you would most like to use in your future work.

SKILLS WITH INFORMATION

Synthesizing - Integrating - Conceiving - Conceptualizing - Innovating

Visualizing - Imagining - Inventing - Discovering - Learning

Selecting - Arranging - Designing - Developing

Brainstorming - Elaborating - Improvising - Reasoning

Organizing - Planning - Implementing - Coordinating - Scheduling

Analyzing - Examining - Evaluating - Appraising - Deciding

Investigating - Researching - Observing - Experimenting - Predicting

Identifying - Gathering - Compiling - Categorizing - Classifying

Interpreting - Translating - Traveling - Articulating

Computing - Calculating - Programming

Copying - Comparing - Correcting - Proofreading

Collecting - Storing - Retrieving - Remembering

Writing - Reporting - Reading - Editing - Composing - Conducting

Adapting - Modifying - Improving - Revising - Simplifying - Reviewing

Anticipating - Clarifying - Intuiting - Understanding - Summarizing

Acting - Clowning - Dancing - Singing - Impersonating - Pantomiming

Purchasing - Budgeting - Financing - Producing

SKILLS WITH PEOPLE

Mentoring - Counseling - Advising - Coaching - Consulting - Guiding

Assessing - Interviewing - Facilitating - Collaborating

Negotiating - Advocating - Mediating - Arbitrating - Debating

Instructing - Teaching - Training - Tutoring - Explaining - Presenting

Communicating - Questioning - Listening - Relating - Empathizing

Speaking - Talking - Signing - Informing - Demonstrating

Supervising - Managing - Directing - Delegating - Monitoring

Leading - Initiating - Competing - Team-building - Recruiting

Entertaining - Amusing - Performing - Dramatizing

Persuading - Influencing - Motivating - Inspiring

Promoting - Selling - Publicizing - Representing - Welcoming

Greeting - Serving - Assisting - Accommodating - Recommending

Helping - Care giving - Caring for animals - Caring for plants

SKILLS WITH THINGS

Painting - Drawing - Sketching - Sculpting - Illustrating

Photographing - Filming - Videotaping - Recording

Applying makeup - Decorating - Crafting - Sewing - Weaving

Setting up - Operating - Controlling - Driving - Navigating

Tending - Handling - Lifting - Moving - Expediting

Building - Assembling - Constructing - Installing

Exhibiting - Displaying - Preparing - Mixing - Measuring

Restoring - Repairing - Remodeling - Refinishing - Preserving

Altering - Adjusting - Inspecting - Testing - Troubleshooting

Engraving - Carving - Chiseling - Molding - Shaping

Playing musical instruments - Puppeteering - Performing magic tricks

Cleaning - Maintaining - Massaging - Tattooing

Coordinating hand-eye - Coordinating body - Modeling

Another talent-finding technique is to ask yourself what others appreciate about you. Think about what other people have thanked you for.[28] Or ask people who know you well what they think you do best. One of my clients did this as homework and sheepishly reported in our next session that everyone remarked that she was a good talker! Her new career became public relations, in part because of that feedback.

You could also download the list of skills from the Career Notebook section of www.creativecareers.com. Give the list to people from different parts of your life, such as family, friends, and coworkers. Have them circle the skills that they think of as your greatest strengths. Then compare their lists with your own. Those skills that show up on all three lists are ones you can count on.

You may be surprisingly blind to your strengths—so close to yourself that you can't see. You may think that because you are good at something, everyone else is, too. Or that if a task comes easily to you, then it's no big deal. Perhaps your strongest skills come so easily and naturally that you are barely aware of using them. It may never have occurred to you that you could earn a good living by doing those things you do so effortlessly.

Originally I considered counseling as a career because people kept suggesting it for me. They knew, better than I, how well I listened. Even now, it is so easy for me to listen, to empathize with other people, that sometimes I don't feel like I'm really working when I am counseling. Occasionally I even feel as though I should be trying harder and putting forth the same kind of effort that I would if I were, say, scrubbing the floor.

Here are some questions to help identify your natural strengths—you will also find these questions as downloadable support tools in the Career Notebook section of my website (www.creativecareers.com)— designed to be used as part of a broader framework for guiding your career choice and job search:

QUESTION #1 What are you doing when you are so engrossed or absorbed or involved that you lose track of time? Brainstorm, write the activities down, and then look for themes or patterns. What do the activities have in common? One client found that he was happiest and most absorbed when he was collecting and organizing things—from beer cans to butterflies. Archiving was a natural career choice for him.

QUESTION #2 In what kinds of activities, relative to yourself and not to others, do you make the boldest choices and take the greatest risks? Very likely it is in those areas that you have the most intuitive confidence in yourself. Again, brainstorm, write down your activities, and look for themes or patterns in your answers. One of my friends was most avant-garde with her clothing. She dressed unlike anybody else and seemed to have a knack for staying one step ahead of fashion. After modeling for a couple of years, she began to design clothing.

QUESTION #3 What are your occupational daydreams? Think about all your work-related daydreams, even those you had when you were a kid. Look for themes in the kinds of work you imagined yourself doing. Take them seriously. One client confessed that he had always dreamed of running off to join the circus and had many fantasies of himself entertaining by juggling, clowning, riding bareback, and walking the high wire. This was very hard for him to admit or act on because his family disapproved of any kind of behavior that they interpreted as "showing off."

QUESTION #4 Another question to consider is how quickly you do certain tasks. Think of your skill in terms of running a race: anyone can cover the distance eventually, but the winner does it the quickest. Those areas in which you work the most quickly, relative to others, are likely to be areas in which you are more skilled. Three broad areas to consider are words, numbers, and images.

To use myself as an example again, I am quick with words. I spoke in sentences early for my age. I can remember friends watching me read in junior high and exclaiming at how fast my eyes were moving! Now almost all my work involves words—reading, writing, speaking, or listening to them. All this communicating provides a good outlet for my high flow of ideas.

On the other hand, my memory for tones is low, at the fifteenth percentile, meaning that out of 100 people, eighty-five of them would have better memory for musical tones than me. Because of this limitation, I was not allowed to play an instrument in elementary school! I never became a musician. But my poor memory for tones has never interfered with my work as a psychologist or writer. It just didn't matter.

I mention both my strengths and my weaknesses because we all have them. People are as different from each other in their abilities as they are in their appearance. Areas of low aptitude can actually be helpful, in that they help you decide what you don't want to do. Although it seems to be human nature to want to be very good at what we do, it's just as legitimate to be bad at something. No one is good at everything.

Of course, you'll do things more quickly with practice—it's not all aptitude. But people tend to prefer those areas in which they have more aptitude and will, over time, attain even greater skill and speed, compared with people who are not so naturally gifted. For example, even though I have had plenty of practice cooking, I don't really enjoy it, and I am amazed at how fast chefs work. Working with food and kitchen utensils, I am slow and tense and eager to be done with it—perhaps because I have poor finger dexterity and legitimately fear that I'm about to chop off a finger. My artist sister, on the other hand, says she finds working with her hands relaxing. Even though she is working meticulously and precisely, she is relaxed and at ease. She has considered such careers as teaching art, illustrating children's books, and painting copies of well-known works under her own name, none of which would suit me.

> "Contentment comes from identifying the gifts you have been given, submitting them to the necessary training, and then engaging them in work."
>
> —ARTHUR F. MILLER

If you do a skills analysis exercise, you will get immediate feedback on your preferred skills. But if you ask yourself the preceding questions about which tasks you do quickly and daringly and in which tasks you lose track of time, don't expect your first answers to be the final answers. Be alert to patterns that emerge as you remember your past, become more aware of your present behavior, and dream of what you'd like to do in the future. Your skills will gradually become clearer, as though you were focusing a camera lens.

THE QUEST FOR CREATIVE OCCUPATIONS

Imagine that you stand before a Realm of Creative Work. You enter this special world in a spirit of exploration to find your most desired occupations. You are in the Artistic region of the work world, with the least structure and the greatest opportunity to do something new and different. Compared to other realms, efforts here are more likely to be directed toward creating beauty and achieving an emotional effect.

Above all, this is a place where people work with ideas. The ideas are varied and complex, instead of routine and simple; the thinking required is abstract and symbolic instead of concrete and literal. The work here requires you to become very involved with information and to bring information together in new products or services. In fact, compared to work in the other five corners of the hexagon, Artistic work requires among the highest aptitudes for color discrimination, finger dexterity, spatial ability, and intelligence.

> "Empires of the future are empires of the mind."
>
> —**WINSTON CHURCHILL**

As the economy has moved from the Industrial Age to the Information Age, we have left an economy based on the production of goods, moved through an economy based on the provision of services, and now appear to be headed toward an economy based on the synthesis of information. The number of workers who labor exclusively with their bodies is growing smaller, replaced by an ever-increasing number of workers laboring mostly with their brains (and maybe their bodies, too!). The tangible products of manufacturing and agriculture have lost ground to the intangible copyrights, patents, and trademarks of intellectual property.

In 1990, at the dawn of the Digital Revolution, futurist writer Alvin Toffler correctly prophesied that knowledge—not land, raw materials, labor, or capital—was the primary resource and base for a new world economy. Data, information, and knowledge would become primary, he said, and those who could work with them would be in demand. "At every step from today, it is knowledge, not cheap labor; symbols, not raw materials, that embody and add value."[29]

According to author and professor Richard Florida, it is not knowledge per se but creativity itself that spurs economic growth. We are members of a new class that he calls the "creative class." He uses the term *class* in the social and economic sense, the same way we might use the familiar term *middle class*. As members of the creative class, it is our economic function to create new content. He defines "the highest order of creative work as producing new forms or designs that are readily transferable and widely useful—such as . . . composing music that can be played again and again."[30]

Florida identified what he called the "super-creative core" (12 percent of the employed population in the United States), composed of engineers and scientists as well as artists and musicians, architects and designers, writers and editors, and teachers and professors. "The key difference between the Creative Class and other classes lies in what they are primarily paid to do. Those in the Working Class and the Service Class are primarily paid to execute according to plan, while those in the Creative Class are primarily paid to create and [they] have considerably more autonomy and flexibility than the other two classes to do so."[31]

What fun! This is exactly the kind of opportunity Artistic types need and deserve. We like reshaping goods and services into new forms that enhance their usefulness or delightfulness. For us, personal development and economic development may at long last be aligned in a new age of opportunity.

Creative work does indeed appear to have entered a new era. For example, in the United Kingdom in 2011, the fields of advertising, architecture, publishing, and writing were thriving in terms of pay and job stability—even better than noncreative disciplines![32] In Australia in 2011, the incomes of creative workers were above the norm, even though 60 percent of them were self-employed. And a huge number of industries—129 in all—employed Australian designers and illustrators.[33]

If you'd like to become part of the "super-creative core," look for ways that you can add value to information so that it benefits others. There are lots of ways to do this, from conducting the Philharmonic to designing a new landscape that enhances already existing structures. New information adds value to already-existing information when it is done in a way that benefits a third party. Products become better products by the addition of ideas, knowledge, and creative skills, including advanced technology. Let's look at some examples.

With the movie *The Princess and the Frog*, the creative people at Walt Disney Studios took a well-known story (the "information" in this case) and added value to it in many different ways. Writers developed the story and wrote a screenplay; cartoonists created and animated characters; actors and actresses provided voices; artists designed backgrounds and special effects; composers and lyricists wrote an original score; instrumental musicians and singers performed the songs; directors and editors brought it all together into a pleasing whole.

Creative people add value in other ways as well. For example, some fashion stylists now offer online services, selecting clothing for their customers to try on and approve. Some chefs plan menus and set up ingredients and kitchen equipment so their customers can quickly prepare nutritious meals for home use. My brother-in-law, an economist, adds value to an unwieldy mass of data provided by the government. By selecting the most relevant data, analyzing it with appropriate software, and organizing it according to economic principles, he tailors economic information to the unique needs of each of his clients.

Since the previous edition of this book, the floodgates have opened, enabling creative content to flourish online. For example, bloggers can support themselves by independently adding value to information, without needing to first be accepted or edited by someone from the publishing industry. Here's a summary observation from *Makers: The New Industrial Revolution*, a book written by Chris Anderson:

> "*The greatest change of the past decade has been the shift in time people spend consuming amateur content instead of professional content.*

The rise of Facebook, Tumblr, Pinterest, and all the others like them is nothing less than a massive attention shift from the commercial content companies of the twentieth century to the amateur content companies of the twenty-first."[34]

BACK TO SKILLS AGAIN

Your favorite skills can help orient you to the world of work. At one time, the U.S. Department of Labor analyzed occupations in three categories: (1) skills with information, (2) skills with people, and (3) skills with things. The results of some formal skills analyses are already organized in this way. If you haven't done a formal analysis but you did ask yourself the earlier questions about skills (on pages 60 to 62), take a look at your answers and see if your skills fall mostly into the ideas, people, or things categories.

If you are unsure, ask yourself how involved you want to be with ideas, people, and things. In other words, how closely or intimately do you want to work with ideas or people or things? If you still don't know, begin with those categories for which you have the greatest patience. Conversely, avoid those that require you to deal with whatever you find the most exasperating, such as difficult people or broken things.

One of my clients originally thought that she wanted to teach French, an occupation that requires higher-level skills with both ideas and people. However, after teaching junior high for a while, she discovered that she was too thin-skinned and sensitive, easily upset when students were rude or disinterested. After analyzing her preferred skills, she realized that what she really wanted was to work more closely with ideas and less closely with people. She found success working as an editor for a publisher of foreign language textbooks.

Keep in mind that you don't need to restrict yourself to only ideas or people or things. Some careers, like teaching art or music, require high-level skills with all three. You might also want to choose different kinds of work requiring different skills. In my case, I wanted to work with ideas all the time and people about half the time, which I could accomplish as a writer and a part-time psychologist. On the other hand, because I didn't want to work with things more than I had to, I didn't even look in that direction for my career.

Now let's explore occupations. Because we are in a realm of ideas, each of the three primary territories involves ideas (or information) to some degree. You can head down the path that involves ideas almost exclusively, or the path that involves ideas and people, or the path that involves ideas and things.

THE THREE PATHS

1. The Ideas Path

Writers - Directors - Performers - Investigators - Coordinators - Evaluators - Promoters - Collections Organizers - Language Converters - Models

2. The Ideas and People Path

Mentors - Negotiators - Instructors - Supervisors - Entertainers - Persuaders

3. The Ideas and Things Path

Designers - Image Makers - Photographers - Performers - Electronic Designers - Supervisors - Finishers - Model Builders - Food Preparers - Restorers

The three paths branch off in different directions, toward smaller groups of occupations. These groups have been organized by a primary skill, increasing the chance that you will recognize those skills that you most enjoy using when you see them all together. For example, on the Idea Path, all the occupations in the group of Writers require skill with writing (including writing music). Under Directors you'll find occupations that require directing the creative work of others. All occupations listed under Coordinators require the coordination of a sequence of activities, and so on.

Once you've surveyed the three paths in the preceding section and found your preferred skills, turn to the Career Reference Section at the back of the book (page 157) and begin reading about those occupations. Among them you should find several that are interesting and appealing to you. Each entry describes the kind of work done in that occupation as well as possible employers. Median salaries are included for the more common occupations.

The Career Reference Section contains 281 occupations whose Holland codes have an A in either the first or second place, meaning that they ought to be Artistic enough to appeal to creative and unconventional people. Many of these occupations came from the third edition of the *Dictionary of Holland Occupational Codes.*[35] To these I have added occupations from other sources, including the O*NET. Most of the codes you'll see were provided by research, but I created some codes for new occupations and changed a few existing codes that seemed wrong to me, based on my understanding. So please bear this in mind.

As you look through the occupations in the Career Reference Section, you will notice that many of them are marked by an arrow ➡ and some by a square ■ symbol.

The ➡ indicates an occupation that permits the worker to use the very highest level of skill in working with information: synthesizing. Synthesizing means integrating information, bringing parts together to create a new whole. So if you have lots of ideas and want to choose work with the best opportunity to exercise your creativity, pay special attention to those occupations marked by an arrow.

The ■ symbol indicates careers that are not on the Things trail that may nevertheless require a high level of skill with things.

NOW WHAT?

Many career adventurers feel a little anxious at this point. There is something slightly unnerving about staying open and considering so many options. The good news is that we aren't going to open things up much further. Now we will begin to narrow down your options to the best ones.

Let's presume that you feel ready to move toward making a career decision. What do you do? (The materials available in the Career Notebook section at www.creativecareers.com can be used as support tools for the following steps.) Here are my recommendations, in order:

1. Make a list of three to nine occupations that are most attractive to you. You don't need to find an exact match with your three-letter code, but you might eliminate from further consideration those that don't provide a decent overlap. If your code is AIR, for example, then SAE occupations would probably not be close enough, but IAR or RAI or AIC occupations would be worth looking into.

2. Once you have narrowed down to several possibilities, learn more about them. It's time to do some research! A good place to start is the Internet. My Recommended Websites page at www.creativecareers.com will help you get started. One website well worth visiting is O*NET (www.onetonline.org). O*NET stands for Occupational Information Network, an online source of job information and tools.

You can use the O*Net website to both narrow down and also get more information. First, click on Skills Search and select your preferred skills. When you then click on Find Occupations, you will be presented with a list of occupations that require your selected skills. The O*NET Summary Report for each occupation includes a list of skills, abilities, and work activities, which you can use to rule out or confirm your choices. You will also find Holland code information in their Interests category.

Don't forget the public library! Give your job titles to the career librarian or reference librarian and ask for help locating more information. Begin by reading general information; if that appeals, then move on to more specific information. A great beginning reference is the *Occupational Outlook Handbook,* which offers very accessible information, often easier to read than the O*Net. Published by the U.S. Department of Labor, it, too, is online at www.bls.gov/ooh.

3. When you have learned as much as possible through print or electronic media, talk to people who do that kind of work. Ask them the questions that haven't been answered by your reading. Your goal is to find out what the job is like, so that you can determine whether you would enjoy it. You can also ask the people you interview for names of other people to talk to. I recommend that you interview at least three people who are employed in the occupation that you are researching, to gain a broader perspective.

By asking people about their career paths, you can better understand what it really takes to excel in an industry, what qualifications are required, and whether the field is growing. You can also get firsthand insights about what the interviewees like and dislike about their work. This information can save you from wasting time and money pursuing a career path that is not right for you. On the flip side, it can affirm if you are on the right track.

4. By now you will have learned enough to know that many of the options are not for you. Reject them. That makes your list shorter, which is a sign of progress. Now it is time to get some firsthand experience with the final few contenders. You might volunteer to do a project. You might also join the appropriate professional association or simply visit the meetings of local chapters.

Try tapping into your network in order to create a job-shadow experience. If you need assistance, university career counseling offices and local Workforce Centers may be able to help you find employers in need of interns. Networking plays a key role in finding job-shadow opportunities, internships, and paid positions, as well as in making connections and building community with others who share similar creative interests.

5. When you are ready, take some time to think about the advantages and disadvantages of your remaining options. Your final career choice won't be so much right or wrong as it will have positive and negative consequences. What are the pros and cons of each option? Whether you prefer to use reason or intuition as your final guide, your decision will likely be enhanced by thinking in advance about the pros and cons.

6. Make a choice. Now that you are informed about your options, reason, intuition, or a combination of both will help you decide. Even if you are really excited about only one option, keep an alternate in mind. Sometimes things don't work out as you had hoped, and it truly helps your peace of mind to know that you have an attractive alternative. I know this from personal experience! And keep in mind that making a career change (or several) is becoming quite common, especially as we live and work longer. There's no need to feel that you must make one choice now for your entire working life.

7. Look for a job or find appropriate training. Once you have determined what you want to do, you must find an employer who needs someone to do just that. Present yourself to such employers as the person who will solve their problem. That's a little simplistic, of course. Volumes have been written about the art of job hunting. For all the details, consult a job-hunting classic like *What Color Is Your Parachute?* If you would prefer to job hunt via the Internet, a recommended website, considered by many to be the gateway site, is www.rileyguide.com.

JOB TITLES

Let's consider the advantages and disadvantages of using job titles. The nice thing about job titles is that people like them. They are so definite and graspable that they lend security to both speaker and listener. Job titles can be useful and save you a paragraph of job description. When you are doing your own investigation into the jobs that appeal to you most, it's helpful to know what people in the field call themselves, so you can make a better first impression by speaking their language.

The problem with job titles is that the work world is very fluid. Organizing information by job titles, as I have done here, gives you the impression that different occupations are crisp and neat and do not overlap. However, as you will quickly learn, that impression is misleading. Let me give you some examples. There are few people earning a living as full-time color experts, but there are many graphic designers or interior designers who do the work of a color expert as part of their jobs. There are few bona-fide fashion coordinators, but a variety of sales promoters in the fashion industry do some fashion coordination.

On the other hand, some occupations combine the work of a number of job titles. An independent filmmaker, for example, does the work of a scriptwriter, set designer, camera operator, director, editor—and sometimes even actor! Instructional design can include some of the work done by trainers, graphic designers, computer artists, media production specialists, and instructional material directors. The point is to use job titles when they help you but not let yourself get boxed in.

IF NONE OF THESE ARE FOR YOU

If you have looked over the 281 creative occupations listed in the Career Reference Section and none of them please you, here are some suggestions.

Don't expect to be hit by a thunderbolt. I have never once seen a career client go into ecstasy over an option we turned up during counseling. Only once did a young man literally hurry out the door because he was so excited that he couldn't wait to begin. If anything, people seem more likely to resist their best and most natural choices.

It may be premature for you to be thinking about specific occupations. If you are younger—say, in your twenties—and not yet established in a career, the best first step for you

> "Even trash can be picked up artistically."
>
> —**FRED ASTAIRE**

may be to choose a field. (See the list of fields on page 16.) Fields are more stable than occupations, and they have other advantages as well. You can change jobs more easily within the same field, and any work you do in that field adds to your expertise. So, for example, if advertising is your field, but you're just starting, then you can look for temp work in advertising agencies, where at least you'll be learning about your new area and getting some relevant experience while you hunt for a better job or get additional training.

The best career decision I ever made was my decision to go into psychology when I was twenty-six years old. Since that time, I have been paid to work as an instructor, a therapist, an evaluator, a supervisor, a keynoter, a writer, a researcher, and so on, all in the field of psychology. I've been paid by public schools and universities and private clients and publishers and so forth. My field has given me a lot of latitude to learn about new areas, to be creative, and to jump ship when I get bored. And I still like it!

In our crazy and insecure work world in which companies are sold or merged or downsized almost overnight, and hiring and firing happen faster than ever before, you may find it helpful to look to your field or discipline or profession as a more stable source of identity. Jobs and employers may come and go, but your loyalty and dedication to literature or the environment can remain intact. Individuals these days take less pride in their employer and more pride in the identity that comes from their discipline and lifestyle.

If neither occupational titles nor fields appeal to you, try themes. Themes are a different way to label your motivated abilities. The book *Strengths Quest: Discover Your Strengths in Academics, Career, and Beyond* describes thirty-four themes based on Gallup's research with millions of individuals.[36] You might be able to determine your strengths from reading the book, or you might prefer to take their online assessment (www.strengthsquest.com; a $10 access code is required), which provides you with a signature list of your highest five themes. Be forewarned that once you know your themes, they will not point directly to any particular occupation.

Another alternative is to take the Self-Directed Search, either by ordering it from Psychological Assessment Resources (800-331-TEST) or paying online at www.self-directed-search.com. Either way, you can review many possible occupations suggested by your three-letter Holland code. You may find occupations with an A as the third letter of their Holland codes that appeal to you. One of my clients found that working as a leasing consultant for a real estate developer was a great fit for her. She felt like an actress, putting on a show as she presented apartments to new people every day. Not only did she enjoy the variety and autonomy of the job, but she also loved spending much of her day outdoors and avoiding office politics.

I certainly don't want to give the impression that occupations classified as Artistic in Holland's scheme are the only creative ways to work. In fact, Artistic occupations are simply the ones that provide the best outlet for creative self-expression. They allow you to blend beauty and truth, thinking and feeling. Science and engineering provide the best outlet for a different, more objective kind of creativity. It is certainly possible to have creative politicians and accountants and ranchers, to name a few other examples. A person can be creative in any field. All fields may not permit the worker quite as much latitude to do the work in new and different ways, but they undoubtedly allow enough latitude for creative contributions.

This chapter has been about abilities and skills, as the last chapter was about interests and personality. If you don't resonate with the occupations provided and you are still unsure what to do, the most simple and important steps are to (1) identify an area of interest and (2) identify a skill or two. From there you can conduct your own investigation into possible creative work that may not be described in the usual sources. The creative occupations listed at the back of this book are the most traditional. There are more possibilities, but you will have to work harder to find them.

> "The creative act is not an act of creation in the sense of the Old Testament. It does not create something out of nothing; it uncovers, selects, reshuffles, combines, synthesizes already existing facts, ideas, faculties, skills. The more familiar the parts, the more striking the new whole."
>
> —**ARTHUR KOESTLER**

Let me provide a few examples. Suppose you are interested in different cultures and you have skill with mediating. You may discover an emerging occupation: cultural mediator. Cultural mediators help resolve communication difficulties among people of different cultures. Or maybe you are interested in art and skilled with advising. You could become an art advisor, helping individuals and organizations find and select fine art for purchase. Someone interested in training might find work using their computer gaming skills to create a more holistic educational environment for business employees.

With diligent investigation, you can discover possibilities for your own unique combination of interests and abilities. You could even create your own unconventional career—something that has never been done before or a combination of existing jobs that is uniquely yours. For more on this, see the next chapter.

Chapter 4
COMPOSE YOUR OWN CAREER

In the last chapter we explored the realm of creative occupations; in this chapter we'll consider different options for arranging work into a lifestyle that provides for both creative expression and financial survival. Just as writers and musicians and artists choose aesthetic elements and arrange them in an original composition, you can choose creative pursuits along with other endeavors and arrange them in your own unique support structure.

Before we even consider more options, maybe our first step is to acknowledge that there are risks involved. Any career adventure is a risky undertaking, because job security has gone the way of the dinosaurs. Even so-called full-time, permanent positions can disappear in a heartbeat. Virtually any job in today's workplace is nothing more than a temporary assignment. Whether we work for an employer or for ourselves, job security has become our responsibility, requiring that we "own" and "manage" our own careers.

In other words, the old plight of creative people has become the new normal. No longer are Artistic types the only ones who must grapple with temporary employment. Engineers and health care professionals, for example, are increasingly being offered contract work and per diem employment, rather than full-time opportunities. People who need to be in continual job search mode are therefore creating multiple streams of income so they are not caught flat-footed when a position ends unexpectedly. Whether you are a painter, a poet, or even a software engineer, it is good career management to develop secondary income sources, thereby creating a greater sense of security for yourself.

What's the good news? There is more freedom than ever before. Unconventional people often adapt well to a changing world without rules. Rather than bemoaning the loss of the conventional lifetime job with a single employer, we actually appreciate the freedom and flexibility provided by taking an unconventional approach. Let's take a closer look at how you can use your freedom to integrate your personal and professional lives into a more meaningful and creative whole.

Confucius said, "Do what you love, and you will never have to work a day in your life." Do you agree? CEO and business writer Patty Azzarello doesn't. She claimed in 2010: "'Do what you love' is bad advice. . . . The number of people who make a lot of money doing what they love is so insignificantly small that it's an unrealistic and useless thing to model. The most unfortunate thing about this is that it makes people feel like they are failing when they don't achieve it." Instead, she advocates working for money and doing what you love for free.[37]

The views of Confucius and Azarello anchor two ends of a continuum. We'll use that continuum to order different ways you can support yourself, roughly according to the time available to do what you love the most. You might use just one, several, or all eight routes at different times in your life. You can move fluidly from one to another as circumstances change, and you can use more than one route at a time.

Here are eight different options from which you can pick and choose to compose your own career:

1. Create an unconventional career.
2. Get a grant or find a patron.
3. Take a creative job as a way to earn your living.
4. Freelance a service.
5. Teach in your field.
6. Run a small business marketing your creative work.

7. Take a conventional job and have a creative hobby.

8. Take a bread-and-butter job to support your creative ambitions temporarily, until your creative work is self-supporting.

Now let's look at the real-life compositions of some creative people who have followed these eight options.

CAREER OPTION ONE:
CREATE AN UNCONVENTIONAL CAREER

Dana Smith's very unconventional career began in 1974 when he left college to join a small traveling circus. The circus turned out to be the perfect platform from which to launch his forty-year career as a solo street performer. Dana still works as a street performer, and he also does fee-for-service gigs at university campuses, park and recreation departments, state fairs, festivals, and all-inclusive resorts around the United States, as well as in Canada and Mexico.

Dana believes part of his success came from being in the right place at the right time. There was a movement happening in San Francisco in which performers and artisans were figuring out how to earn a living by doing what they loved. According to Dana, "We were providing practical, affordable art and entertainment. I was one of many artists trying to prove the model that we could pay our bills, move ourselves forward, and sustain a living. Still, there were major sacrifices of material things in our quest for doing good work."

Beyond adaptability, what does it take to follow your heart and make a living doing what you love for forty years? Dana's approach to creating art and making business decisions is one part imagination, one part intuition, and one part action. "A soloist needs to be able to tap into their dream factory for ideas. They also need to pick from their imagination the elements that are most actionable. Then, you need to trust your intuition in order to act without wasting time or going down too many dead ends. A sole proprietor can learn from others, but they need to be able to determine for themselves the most practical and efficient way forward."

Dana adds, "That has been the tricky part of my career. I have never known exactly how going forward will look or how it will turn out. I only know that as I am willing to go forward and take action, the world has met me and answered. Ask the world and give people a way to respond to your requests. When I find myself getting stuck, I choose the most efficient way forward and take action."

Dana talks about stepping out to do a show when the air is warm and the whole world feels lush and vibrant. "The audience is right there with me, fully engaged. It is electric. Inspirational. As a performer, I live for those warm, sunlit August evenings. People often come up to me after one of those shows asking how they can do what I do for a living. People want to think that every day of your life is this August day! What most people seem to forget is that we all need to endure a fair number of cold, rainy days in February in order to do the work we love. We need to be honest with ourselves, and admit that as artists, doing anything else makes us so crazy that we can barely endure being here on earth! As artists, we will put up with obstacles and challenges in order to capture those moments that are like that sunlit August afternoon."

Ever evolving, Dana has written three novels and is now creating a new show platform, "The Novel Juggler" (www.danasmith.com). Whether you find him on the pavement or on the page, Dana's unconventional career is strong evidence that if we are willing to leap, the net really will appear.

CAREER OPTION TWO:
GET A GRANT OR FIND A PATRON

Another way to pursue your creative work is to get a grant or find a patron. Foundations, corporations, and government arts councils offer grants in virtually every creative field. With a bit of research, it is possible to find grant opportunities in your specific area of interest. Chapter 5 has more information on getting grants and locating other kinds of public support.

Carolyn Wadley Dowley lives in Perth, Australia. She is married and the mother of three children. In 2013, Carolyn received a $40,000 grant from the Australian Arts Council to continue her work on a historical nonfiction book. Carolyn had completed the research phase of the project and was working on the manuscript when she applied for and won the grant.

Carolyn says, "I was an architect in my former life, before writing." She began reading Australian history in her spare time. She became intrigued about a little known bit of Australian history and she began doing research. "Happily, I found a thesis supervisor in the history department at the university who did not think it strange for an architect to turn their hand to writing. He showed a great and sustaining faith in me and my ideas and encouraged me to pursue the impossible as if it were possible."

Even as she made the transition to her new career, Carolyn received a scholarship enabling her to give up her income as an architect, go back to school to earn a master's degree in Australian studies, and eventually write and publish her first book. *Through Silent Country* was published in 2000 and soon after won a national history award.

Carolyn found funding to support her writing, not once, but twice. "Being selected as a 2013 grant recipient was incredible. I had, of course, anticipated that being given the money would be pretty fabulous! The financial support would make a big difference to my work, freeing my hours to be able to write. What I hadn't imagined, though, was the amazing impact of knowing that I had been chosen, that my project had been selected from the hundreds that the council looked at—it was incredibly affirming."

Carolyn is passionate about her work. The stories she is bringing forth are compelling, and she strongly believes that "new" historical knowledge will promote a deeper understanding among Australians. Carolyn adds, "The grant reminds me that other people are waiting for the book to be finished. They believe in it!"

While receiving a grant is an incredible honor, there are certain pressures that come with the opportunity. Carolyn says, "The timeline is a challenge. My background as an architect gave me valuable experience in project management. I broke the project into manageable pieces with deadlines along the way." At the time of this writing, Carolyn was slightly ahead of schedule. She says, "That is a good feeling!" Her final words of encouragement are quite simple: "Believe in yourself and your idea. Dream your dream—it's not impossible!"

CAREER OPTION THREE:
TAKE A CREATIVE JOB

For many people it makes the most sense to take a full-time job doing creative work for an employer. Jason Skowronek is currently an art director at The Children's Place, a children's clothing store chain with 1,500 locations in the United States and abroad. He works in the marketing department at corporate headquarters in New Jersey, overseeing the graphic design of all in-house and window-display graphics.

Jason graduated from college in 2003 with a degree in graphic design from Central Saint Martin's University of the Arts in London, England. He studied graphic design and illustration. "I really appreciate that my degree was very conceptual and arts based, as opposed to vocationally focused. You can gain trade skills on the job, but it is hard to learn the fine art or conceptual side on your own," he says.

"It was after graduation that I really honed my graphic design skills. I learned more about typography and graphic design software programs through a series of internships with several advertising agencies and small graphic design firms." Jason worked as a freelancer for two and a half years before taking his current position. He even did project work for The Children's Place, which allowed him to get a taste of the culture before accepting a full-time job offer.

Jason appreciates the financial rewards and paid vacation that come with having a permanent position. "I like the regiment of the day that involves waking up and commuting on a regular schedule. I need that structure. When I was freelancing, I was constantly working long hours and worrying about getting the next job lined up. When you get very busy on a project, you don't have time to be seeking out the next paying client," he adds.

"Now my job is very much 9 to 5. Our team produces a lot of designs, but at the end of the day I can leave my work at the office. This allows me time to pursue other interests. I teach a graphic design course at a local college every fall. I also do occasional freelance work, which allows me to continue to develop my portfolio and to inspire creativity within myself."

Jason does not take his career for granted. "I feel so lucky to be in a creative job. It is amazing that I can make a living doing what I do. I really enjoy working with other creative people every day. We egg each other on to do better work all the time, which keeps it from getting stagnate and boring. As an art director as well as in my role as a teacher, I have the opportunity to inspire others to do art and be creative."

CAREER OPTION FOUR:
FREELANCE A SERVICE

Freelance work is a way of working for a variety of companies or clients at different times, as opposed to being "permanently" employed by a single employer. The decision to freelance can be economically or artistically driven; many times it is both. However, as the workplace has changed, the line between permanent employment and freelancing has become blurry. It is increasingly common for people to have multiple streams of income.

This trend is reflected in employment surveys. Employment experts predict that 40 percent of the workforce will be made up of contingent or independent workers by 2020.[38] Some experts believe the percentage is much higher when you take into account the millions of people with so-called "permanent" jobs who simultaneously freelance.

As mentioned earlier in this chapter, more and more companies are hiring contingent and independent workers on a contract basis to perform certain tasks and complete specific projects. In my experience, many contractors and consultants are actually job seekers looking for their next "permanent" employment opportunities. In other words, many people freelance or work independently to get by during a career transition, with a goal of moving back into more stable employment as soon as they can. This is quite different from making a conscious decision to freelance because you want to be your own boss.

Not everyone enjoys selling their products or services, so it can be important to understand your personality and your needs when considering how to best arrange your career. How can you determine if a freelance career is right for you?

First, freelancers tend to prefer a flexible schedule. In addition to flexible hours, they may want the freedom to work from a variety of locations. Second, many creative and artistic types get bored in regular jobs in which they do the same things over and over. Freelancing may be the right path for you if you are inspired and energized by tackling a variety of projects, and if you enjoy having creative control over your work. You may also want to consider freelancing if office politics and corporate cultures leave you feeling stressed out and drained.

With these criteria in mind, you may choose to make a giant leap into a freelance career. Or, you might instead take small steps in this direction until your freelance income becomes sustainable. Ultimately, freelancing may comprise your entire career or remain just something extra you do on the side.

Marcella Wells is an example of someone who initially came to freelancing more as a way of coping with career adversity than by choice. It has taken some time but she now feels a huge sense of accomplishment and gratification in her career as an evaluator, planner, and educator specializing in creating high-impact interpretive programs and exhibits in both indoor and outdoor learning environments, such as museums, national parks, and botanic gardens. Her education includes a bachelor's degree in parks and recreation with a specialty in interpretation, a master's degree in tourism planning, and a doctoral degree in social sciences and natural resource management. The focus of her freelance work is consulting with companies and organizations to plan, evaluate, and enhance the impact of their informal educational programs.

In the past fifteen years, Marcella has completed more than eighty projects in twenty-two states for fifty different organizations. Projects have included everything from researching and writing interpretive labels for exhibits to planning and managing large development projects, such as the Visitor Center at Hoover Dam in Las Vegas.

Having a unique niche and highly specialized area of expertise has helped Marcella grow her freelance career organically. The majority of her work comes through word-of-mouth referrals, teaching workshops, and speaking at conferences. Marcella says, "My radar is always out, listening for how can I help an organization better understand the impact of what they do. I continually listen for opportunities, and I am not afraid to approach someone directly when I see a potential need I can fill. I have also done a certain amount of pro bono work for organizations, which has led to paid contracts."

Marcella has built a strong network as a freelance consultant. She is an active member of professional associations and has frequently taken on board positions in order to follow policy and industry trends. She considers it vital to maintain and nurture professional relationships. Like many freelancers, Marcella loves the continual learning and the variety of projects. She also appreciates the freedom and flexibility that comes from being her own boss.

At the same time, Marcella acknowledges some of the common challenges of freelancing. "I don't always know where my next project will come from, and I don't always enjoy the tasks associated with marketing myself or managing the financial side of my business." She emphasizes the importance of surrounding yourself with people who can support areas of weakness. It is often better to hire an accountant or website developer rather than struggle to do everything on your own.

Successful freelancing requires having passion for the work you do. Marcella says, "What still gives me chill bumps is getting a call from a potential client who has a problem and asks if I can help them. My mind immediately starts thinking of possibilities, and I am off and running on a new project." It may sound like a cliché, but you must love what you do and produce consistently exceptional work in order to build a lasting career as a freelancer or independent consultant.

CAREER OPTION FIVE:
TEACH IN YOUR FIELD

Teaching is a great way to share your talents with the world, especially if you have a Social streak. There are so many different ways to teach. Teaching can be a small part of what you do to earn a living, or it can be the focus of your career. You can teach any age group; you can be a professional trainer, teaching almost any subject, or you can be a subject-matter expert, teaching only about your area of expertise; you could be self-employed or work for an educational institution or for a training company.

Nicole Wilshusen is a music therapist and full-time assistant professor in the Music Therapy Department at Colorado State University in Fort Collins. Nicole teaches piano classes for music-therapy majors. She also teaches the Introduction to Music Therapy course, supervises practicum students, and coordinates their practicum experiences.

After earning a bachelor's degree in music therapy, Nicole began working with developmentally disabled students in an elementary school setting. She later worked in hospice and with elderly patients in nursing homes. While establishing herself in the field, she found it necessary to supplement her income by offering private piano lessons, teaching parent-toddler music classes, and even taking part-time jobs outside her field. Throughout her career, she has worked with private clients as well.

Nicole says, "I enjoy working one-on-one with clients, but I always knew that private practice wasn't my path. It takes a long time to build a successful practice. I don't enjoy the pressure of needing to drum up business. I prefer working for an organization, so that I don't have to manage the other tasks related to running a practice."

Initially, Nicole dismissed teaching as a possible career path. However, when she went back to school to earn her master's degree in music therapy, she accepted a graduate teaching assistant position. She quickly discovered that she really enjoyed working with the students, developing curriculums, and finding creative ways to deliver lessons. "After graduation, a part-time teaching position opened up in the music therapy department. I have now been a full-time assistant professor for the past four years. The position is a great fit for me."

Nicole enjoys the flexibility of teaching. She also enjoys the steady paycheck, health benefits, academic breaks, and paid time off that comes with working in higher education. Nicole remembers the early days of her career, when she put in twelve-hour days, juggling part-time jobs and private piano lessons to make ends meet. As she began raising a family, she wanted a more stable income and flexible schedule.

"I really love what I do. The students come into the program with their own backgrounds and experiences. Many have personal stories that inspired them to study music therapy. I appreciate their passion and it helps keep me passionate, too." Nicole adds, "Teaching allows me to have a bigger impact in the world. It is exciting to know that I have helped educate a student who is now doing amazing work in the field."

CAREER OPTION SIX:
RUN A SMALL BUSINESS

Running your own small company is generally considered one of the most daring career paths of all. It can be a risky, high-stakes adventure fraught with never-ending challenges. It can also be incredibly rewarding. People often shy away from going into business for themselves because they think a regular job offers greater security (although many corporate refugees disagree!). Running a small business may be perfect for you if you have strong enterprising qualities and an entrepreneurial spirit.

Barry Wachtel has owned and operated his own interior design company for forty years. He has had hundreds of employees along the way. Today, he is easing into retirement and works independently for select clients. He says, "Running a business is constantly challenging, but that is what I love about it. I was not tied to an employer who created scenarios for me. I have been able to create my own game plan."

In the beginning, his company designed and manufactured custom cabinetry. Today, Barry focuses on complete interior architecture and design. This includes selecting the front door and designing virtually everything inside a home. Numerous project pages on the Houzz website (www.houzz.com/user/bwinteriors) offer a glimpse into Barry's gift for creating beautiful living spaces.

Barry acknowledges that a good part of his success was driven by his desire to play in his own playground. "I had to work really hard so that I would not have to work for someone else. And, there were sacrifices along the way. I sacrificed time with family, and it took a long time before I was making a good living. People are always looking for security. But there are some crazy people for whom security is not the first motive. An entrepreneur needs to be able and willing to ride the highs and lows while they establish a successful business."

Running a small business does not always mean taking on employees. Many "soloprenuers" work for themselves, all by themselves. Kat Williams is a full-time, professional blogger from the UK (www.rocknrollbride.com). Her blog offers alternative wedding inspiration and has grown from being "just another bride blog" to one of the most successful, income-generating blogs in the world.

Kat believes the first step to successful blogging, or running any other successful business for that matter, is figuring out what makes you different and clearly defining your target audience. "When you work in a saturated market, you need to be unique in order to avoid fading into the background. You also need to be passionate about your topic." What gets Kat up every morning is "inspiring brides and grooms-to-be to plan the wedding they really want, in a world dictated by tradition and big froufrou dresses."

Other success factors include a willingness to work hard and the ability to continually innovate. Quite prolific, Kat posts new material one or two times a day, which is standard in the wedding blog arena. According to Kat, "Competition is so fierce that you constantly have to be innovating or else you will be left behind."

Kat works long hours from her home office, and most of her social interaction happens online or over the phone. Kat stresses, "Don't quit your day job to become a full-time blogger. It took three years before I started making money. It is definitely not a get-rich-quick scheme."

For Kat, the good definitely outweighs the bad. "I have never done anything else I was this passionate about. I get amazing feedback and validation from my readers who send me pictures and stories about their weddings. And, despite the sacrifices and hard work, I love being my own boss."

In addition to Rock n Roll Bride, Kat and two business partners have formed The Blogcademy to teach others how to blog for a living. Kat offers some final encouragement to those who dream of freelance writing or blogging: "Stop procrastinating! Don't worry if your website is not perfect or if you are unsure of your branding. Just get going, make some mistakes, and figure things out as you go."

CAREER OPTION SEVEN:
HAVE A CREATIVE HOBBY

Another approach to a fulfilling life is to take a non-Artistic job and develop a creative hobby. Sometimes hobbies turn into careers, but then again, not everyone wants their creative pursuits to become moneymaking endeavors. Feeling pressured to make money and please a client might ruin all your fun!

For many people, hobbies offer a wonderful outlet and provide a welcome balance in their lives. No matter how much we love our work, it is unrealistic to expect any job to fulfill all of our needs and desires. Making time for the pursuit of hobbies and interests outside of work can keep you connected to your own creative spirit, as well as to a community of others with similar interests.

Art Siegel is an employment attorney in private practice in San Francisco. He represents employees in workplace and employment disputes. Art has been practicing law for nearly thirty years. In his free time, he is an accomplished photographer.

> "I feel more confident and more satisfied when I reflect that I have two professions and not one. Medicine is my lawful wife and literature is my mistress. When I get tired of one I spend the night with the other. Though it's disorderly, it's not so dull, and besides, neither really loses anything through my infidelity."
>
> —ANTON CHEKHOV

Art began taking pictures at an early age, and he even had a darkroom in his house when he was in junior high school. After working in community theater and filmmaking, he eventually decided to pursue a career in the law, and his creative aspirations slowly fell to the wayside. Art thought practicing law would provide the financial means to support his creative endeavors. However, he found it challenging to stay connected to his artistic pursuits. "When you leave college, you often move away from the community and structures that support creativity."

After a long hiatus, Art began taking pictures again. "With the rise of digital photography, better equipment became cheaper. Suddenly there was the ability to take pictures and see results without having to have the film developed. Online sites such as Flickr and Fotolog came along. This allowed photographers to create online galleries, attract followers, and get feedback about their work. The social networking aspect of photography helped me feel a sense of community with others who shared my interest in the art form."

Art's photographs capture light and shadow, nature and humanity, heart-stopping beauty, and even silly images that offer uncommon glimpses of life (www.flickriver.com/photos/artolog/popular-interesting/). "I have had my work featured in exhibits and I have sold photography. Still, this is not something I would want to make a living doing. That would require developing a whole lot of skills that I don't have, and marketing my work would not be fun at all."

On the other hand, Art admits that if he did not have a creative outlet, he would probably be depressed. "There is not a lot of overlap between my work and my hobby. Photography puts me into an entirely different state of mind. You have to make time for it. It is a fairly solitary pursuit unless I am with a Meet Up group on a photo stroll. I tend to go out alone, get my mind into a creative space, and concentrate on the world around me. It is a source of rich happiness in my life."

CAREER OPTION EIGHT:
TAKE A BREAD-AND-BUTTER JOB

People who want to do creative work often need to work at another job until they establish themselves. A day job works well for many people and is especially well suited to our current job market. Temporary agencies can help you find such work. You might want to work part time, gradually decreasing bread-and-butter activities as you begin to make more money on your creative endeavors.

In *The Complete Job-Search Handbook*, Howard Figler includes a chapter on interim jobs. He lists four criteria for choosing an interim job, acknowledging that it is unlikely you'll find one interim job that meets all four criteria. His criteria are:
1. A large enough income for you and your dependents to live on without great stress.

2. Easily obtainable work that doesn't require years of training and is thus relatively easy for you to take and to leave.

3. Work that makes only moderate demands on your time so that you have time and energy left over for a job search, your creative endeavors, or both.

4. Continuous exposure to a variety of people so you can make contacts during work time and learn about new career opportunities.[39]

> "I've only spent about ten percent of my energies on writing. The other ninety percent went to keeping my head above water."
>
> —KATHERINE ANNE PORTER

> "The best time for planning a book is while you are doing the dishes."
>
> —AGATHA CHRISTIE

Because you may keep your survival job for some time, I would add two other criteria. First, find survival work that fits your personality. Your personality may be mostly Artistic, and you may prefer to do only Artistic work, but your personality is not purely Artistic. You have additional skills and interests that you can parlay into a job. Others have done it: for example, Wallace Stevens was a poet and vice president of an insurance company, T. S. Eliot was a poet and a bank clerk, Spinoza was a philosopher and a lens grinder, and the Wright brothers were inventors and bicycle builders. You don't have to starve in a garret. Barbara Sher recommends that you take a day job you don't hate and call it your "subsidy to the arts"!

Second, it's important to choose work that won't interfere with your psychic life. Some work doesn't fully occupy your mind, leaving you time on the job to mull over aesthetic choices. Other work leaves you so frazzled and stressed that you have trouble turning to your creative projects even when you are off the job. If you don't now know what kinds of work will or won't interfere with your psyche, you will find out through trial and error.

One good book is *150 Jobs You Can Start Today* by Deborah Jacobson.[40] The author knows all about survival work—in fact, she used to support her acting career with a part-time pet-sitting business that she started herself! More suggestions for bread-and-butter work are given below, organized by Holland code. Begin with your most important Holland theme besides Artistic. Look under that theme for day-job ideas. You will find many possible kinds of work you can use to support yourself as you pursue your creative goals.

SOCIAL

Some of the most popular survival jobs for Social types are bartender, security guard, mail carrier, orderly, coffee shop barista, and fast-food worker. More exotic options include detective, comparison shopper, vending-machine attendant, paralegal assistant, traffic school teacher, and employment interviewer.

If you have a Social streak in your personality, consider living in as a companion for an elderly person, a nanny for a young family, a homemaker for busy professionals, a personal assistant for a celebrity, or a home-health aide for someone who is sick. Then you won't even have to pay rent. Or you could take people into your home: become a foster parent or run a boarding house or a bed-and-breakfast. One couple I know created a bed-and-breakfast of unusual charm and beauty. Their artistic flair was expressed in the way they decorated their home and in their presentation of breakfast, afternoon tea, and picnic baskets for their guests.

ENTERPRISING

The largest category of survival work for those with Enterprising skills is in retail sales. There are so many different things to sell—books, cars, pets, china, music, cosmetics, art objects, hearing aids, toys, hardware, computers, and so on. It's possible to sell intangibles, too, such as advertising space, advertising media, educational programs, or vacation packages. Consider sales representative positions in upholstery or furniture repair, water-softening equipment, or elevators and escalators. Or you might design and sell custom closets. Sales jobs often have flexible hours and unstructured work environments, as well as the opportunity to later move into more direct work in a creative industry, assisted by the special knowledge of the market you've gained in sales.

Some of the more popular Enterprising jobs outside of retail sales are telemarketer, fundraiser, manicurist, newspaper carrier, food deliverer, caterer helper, party or event planner, and travel agent. Or you could be a dispatcher for the transportation or public service industries. If you'd like something a little more exotic, consider taking a job as a sightseeing guide, wine steward or stewardess, pool manager, real estate appraiser, interpreter, or private investigator. Or you might manage performing artists as their general manager, stage manager, or tour manager. If you'd like a free apartment, you could work part time as an assistant apartment manager.

INVESTIGATIVE

There are fewer easily accessible Investigative day jobs than any other kind, perhaps because this kind of work often requires years of training. Lab assistant is a general title for Investigative jobs in such diverse places as zoos, hospitals, universities, and research laboratories. Other possibilities include robotics technician, medical or dental lab technician, engineering technician, chemical preparer (compounding chemical ingredients and performing standard tests), line-service attendant (servicing aircraft before flight), and phlebotomist (drawing blood).

REALISTIC

Bread-and-butter work abounds for Artistic types who also have Realistic skills and interests. Some popular interim jobs include janitor, housecleaner, bus driver, truck driver, airport shuttle or limousine driver, messenger, and gardener. More exotic opportunities include massage therapist, fireworks maker, computer service technician, animal caretaker, cabinet maker, picture framer, and specialists who pack and transport musical instruments and equipment for musicians.

General job titles with almost infinite variations are cleaner, drafter, painter, repairer, cook, machine operator, fisher, and laborer. Other job titles include house painter, home repair handyperson, dog and cat food cook, subway or streetcar operator, and nursery farm laborer. For work that may be more aesthetic, consider tailor and custom sewer, cartographer, shoe repairer, tile and marble setter, manicurist, and pedicurist.

The United States has a great shortage of skilled manufacturing workers. In fact, many middle skills jobs are going unfilled because applicants don't have certifications. There is presently a huge need for machinists; for those with the right aptitude and attitude, the job pays very well. If you aren't sure college is for you, consider the skilled trades. Prepare yourself for certification. You may very well find yourself happier and making more money than your counterparts with bachelor of arts degrees.

If it would further your Artistic goals to not have to pay rent, and if you like the country, you might look for a job as a live-in laborer on a farm or ranch. If you'd like a place to live in the city, perhaps you could become a chauffeur or caretaker for owners of multiple homes or executives going overseas. If you would rather be more independent and still earn a decent wage, you might learn a skilled trade—such as that of a carpenter, electrician, plumber, or paper hanger—through a vocational school or apprenticeship. Although such training will take you away from your creative hobby now, it may better help you support your dependents and your creative goals later.

CONVENTIONAL

The most popular survival jobs for those with some Conventional in their personality are waiter or waitress, clerk, cashier, bank teller, directory assistance operator, paralegal, tax preparer, and office temporary worker. Office temps often perform clerical work, such as entering data, alphabetizing files, and answering the phone—any of which could also be done as a Conventional survival job—but with greater flexibility and less commitment.

More unusual choices that are Conventional in nature include library assistant, museum attendant, meter reader, Braille transcriber, proofreader, toll collector, bill collector, building inspector, and groundskeeper. Opportunity should be good for mapping technicians, pharmacy technicians, dental assistants, and medical record technicians.

There are other ways to choose a bread-and-butter job than using your Holland code. You might choose a job because it's in your field, even if the job itself isn't very creative. If you are a visual artist, for example, you might look into work at private art galleries, where you can crate and uncrate paintings, make professional contacts, and learn what happens behind the scenes. Or you could work in an art museum as a tour guide, custodian, guard, or janitor. Or you could assist a well-known artist in his or her studio.

Even if your day job isn't related to your art form, that doesn't mean you have to wait tables! Michelle Dalziel is a talented singer-songwriter in Florida who recently celebrated her one-year anniversary as a massage therapist. She loves helping people, and it makes her happy when people leave her table feeling better. Michelle considers massage therapy her day job even though she sees clients in the evenings. "Massage therapy is incredibly physical. Every client is different, and I must come up with creative approaches to meet their individual needs. The money is good, and it supports my music career."

For the past seventeen years, Michelle and her husband have played mostly original tunes as a duo. She sings and plays guitar and the *djembe,* an African drum. Michelle's favorite venue is a house concert. "People come specifically to hear you. The audience sits in someone's living room and they really listen to your music. I love the intimacy. It is an even exchange of inspiration." She and her husband have recorded numerous CDs. A stroll around their website (dalziel.net) offers a glimpse into this duo's adventurous music career.

Before her career transition, Michelle homeschooled her daughter for many years. When her daughter returned to public school, Michelle decided to go back to school herself, at age forty-four, to study massage therapy. Her goal is to combine music and massage. "I like the balance that the two passions bring to my life."

Michelle credits her bread-and-butter job with reigniting her creativity. "Sometimes when you do something creative for a living, the love for it kind of goes away. You get burned out. Now, I can play music because I want to, not because I need the money." Over the past year, Michelle has found time to start writing songs again. "Massage therapy has given me that freedom. I feel incredibly lucky to be doing the work I am doing both musically and as a massage therapist."

Although we highlighted just one person in each career option, you probably noticed that many of these successful people used several approaches—sometimes simultaneously, sometimes sequentially, changing from one route to another as their interests shifted or their careers blossomed. You, too, can combine strategies. It's your journey.

You might actually increase your financial security by combining strategies. Katy Piotrowski, an award-winning career counselor and author, suggests taking a "muffin tin" approach to your work. In a "muffin tin" approach, you simultaneously pursue a variety of interests and have multiple streams of income. The opposite and more traditional approach looks more like a "loaf" in which you have a single job and do just one thing at a time. The "loaf" approach is becoming less common and less possible in today's world of work.

Many creative folks actually prefer to combine different kinds of work in their careers, because different kinds of work allow them to express different parts of themselves that would be stifled in a single conventional job. If you have several ideas in mind, but you're not sure which to pursue, try them all. Direct experience quickly helps you learn whether you have a knack for a certain kind of work. Be experimental with your career, as an artist is experimental on canvas.

IF YOU ARE STILL NOT SURE WHAT TO DO

One viable choice sometimes overlooked is to redesign your current job. You may be able to get more of what you want in your present position if you negotiate with your employer. For example, you might change your role at work or find ways to increase variety or independence on the job. Or maybe you could work more flexible hours or telecommute. So long as these job redesign options benefit your employer as well as yourself, they might save you the stress of a major transition.

If, however, you feel the call to embark on a full-blown career adventure, it is important to listen to that voice inside that says, "Maybe I *can* do this!" The stories included in this chapter offer proof that it is possible to have a creative career and an authentic lifestyle. These are not the fluffy fairy tales of glossy magazines. Every person featured shared the ups and downs of their journeys. They talked of sacrifice and side jobs and continual challenges. They acknowledged that living the life of your dreams is hard work.

However, their stories should also inspire hope. You will work hard and sacrifice, but at the end of the day, you will have the satisfaction of knowing that you have been true to yourself. This chapter should help you answer that voice inside that asks, "How am I going to make a living doing *that*?" Trust that if even one person in the world is making a living as a blogger or a street performer or whatever it is you dream of doing, then you, too, can follow your dreams.

For those who haven't found their lifestyle answer so far, here's a different take. Career counselor Betsy Brewer distinguished among *job*, *occupation*, *career*, and *vocation* as four separate pathways, which she defined as follows:

A *job* is routine and repetitive and satisfies concrete needs. The benefits of the work—such as pay—are more important than the work itself. Jobs are performed to maintain the status quo, and they require little investment of the personal self.

An *occupation* is a way to obtain material rewards in the role of tax-paying adult. Although plans are short term, the worker feels some affiliation with the organization, contributes to it, and receives in return a sense of identity, purpose, and structure. The occupational role may fit young people just getting started in the work world or more mature workers who want positions that will complement their other, nonpaid activities. In either case, much of the self is preserved for off-duty hours.

> "Your calling is your natural way of being useful."
>
> —LAURENCE BOLDT

> "The secret to life is to put yourself in the right lighting. For some it's a Broadway spotlight; for others, a lamp-lit desk."
>
> —SUSAN CAIN

A *career* will be pursued even after the basic necessities are handled. Careers provide an arena for developing independence and enhancing self-esteem as the worker makes plans, takes initiative, and commits to ongoing productive activity. A career is personally significant and benefits others as well as the self, but careers would not survive unless they fed the worker's ego with group approval.

A *vocation* may not result in financial rewards or social recognition. A vocation is fruitful, process-oriented, mission-centered work that is consonant with one's true nature. The worker is called and sacrifices to answer the call. The whole of the personality is drawn to work in the service of a transcendent purpose. Society benefits and ego is lost as the essential self unfolds, expressing imperfections as well as authentic traits and talents.[41]

According to Brewer, these four pathways are neither sequential nor hierarchical. One is not better than the others, and a worker may be in more than one of these paths at one time. For example, you might take a job as a maid to support your training for a career in public relations. Or you might have an occupation as a technical writer to support your vocation as a screenwriter. If the eight pathways described earlier in the chapter don't appeal to you, you might think about how to compose your career using these four different pathways instead.

What a lot of options: eight different ways to employ your creativity or four different paths for employment. Out of all those different options, how do you pick the best ones?

I recommend that you go with what you *need*. If what you need most right now is the opportunity to realize your creative potential, then make choices that will support that need. If you are a person who really needs structure or stability, then choose accordingly. Maybe all you really need is a good boss for a change. Speaking for myself, I always need a lot of autonomy, and any career choice that lacks autonomy wouldn't last long. Once again, satisfaction follows from knowing ourselves and then getting into an optimal environment.

People are different, and your optimal work environment may be different from someone else's. Some creative people thrive in smaller organizations, where demands are more varied and they can wear different hats and use more of their talents. Other creative people prefer tolerant and flexible work environments, with looser hours and casual dress codes and more freedom to be their freewheeling and innovative selves. Still others might need an organization with plenty of room for advancement or one that allows them to participate in important decisions.

I've had some clients who felt so wounded by their previous employment that my best advice to them, at least for the time being, was to look for a work environment that felt healthy and nurturing. "Forget about the 'perfect job,'" I told them, "until you have healed a bit. Find an organization in which you feel recognized and valued." In fact, many people, especially younger workers, care more about their fit with a company's values, culture, and colleagues than their fit with any particular job: they don't really care what they do, so long as their values align with the organization.

Well, enough about options and choices. It's time to take action. The next two chapters are about turning your choices into important life changes.

PART THREE

MAKING IT HAPPEN

"Even if you're on the right track, you'll get run over if you just sit there!"
—**WILL ROGERS**

Chapter 5
YOU *CAN* GET THERE FROM HERE!

Once you have understood how to match the unique person you are to the world of work, and you have chosen the kind of work or combination of work you want to do, it's time to take action. No one will offer you the unique career you can create for yourself, but you can learn how to make it happen on your own. This chapter contains specific suggestions for how you can set off, stay on track, and keep moving forward in your own career adventure.

Years ago I attended a seminar on creative careers. The speakers were successful professionals from a variety of Artistic occupations—print and broadcast media, public relations, advertising—who had gathered to tell a group of college students how to get into creative fields. They gave tips on the importance of collecting clips to build a portfolio and volunteering or interning as a way to gain experience and meet others. By far the most commonly repeated bit of advice from these successful people to the students was to keep at it—don't give up. "If you want to do creative work like mine," they said, "you've got to persevere."

> "If a man advances confidently in the direction of his dreams, and endeavors to live the life which he has imagined, he will meet with a success unexpected in common hours."
>
> **—HENRY DAVID THOREAU**

Unfortunately, persistence is much easier to advise than it is to accomplish. One cloth designer was so discouraged after three years of trying to sell her exotic silk-screened fabric that she very nearly gave up. But she kept at it—and her fourth year of business was so successful that now she can't keep up with demand. Like this designer, you may find your persistence to be just as important as your talent on the road to success.

The destination itself looks terrific, but it's in the distance. On the road to your goals you may encounter flat tires, detours, wrong turns, and miles of tedium. You move along smoothly for a while, and then life happens. Your relationship breaks up. Your car breaks down. Your relatives need care. Your house needs a new roof. Financial hardship intensifies other stresses. Even if there are no outstanding problems, a tidal wave of maintenance work almost drowns you, and productivity becomes a luxury.

There is no way to prevent the myriad stresses that distract or derail us from our long-range goals. What we need is a way to persist in the resilient pursuit of our favorite possibilities.

> "Nothing in the world can take the place of persistence. Talent will not; nothing is more common than unsuccessful men with talent. Genius will not; unrewarded genius is almost a proverb. Education will not; the world is full of educated derelicts. Persistence and determination are omnipotent. The slogan 'press on' has solved and always will solve the problems of the human race."
>
> **—ATTRIBUTED TO CALVIN COOLIDGE**

Think of this chapter as a short manual to keep you moving forward in your journey. This guide is full of practical tips compiled from therapists and self-help groups like Weight Watchers and Alcoholics Anonymous—people who know what works when it comes to making positive life changes. It is organized into three broad categories of positive coping: using your head, asking for help, and making the most of social media.

USE YOUR HEAD

Heroes are clever. They survive because they keep their wits about them. The following strategies are ones you can practice independently, to keep your career wits about you. As you'll notice, many of these strategies require your heart as well as your head: to stay the course and reach your heart's desire, you will also need to choose and honor your personal values.

SET GOALS

One of the best ways to use your head is to develop an image of what you want in the future. Whether yours is a dream, a vision, a purpose, or a goal, it can be powerfully motivating. Katharine Hepburn did not become a movie star by accident: she wanted to be a star. She aimed high *before* she lived up to her potential.

When I talk to creative people who have been successful in their careers, they tell me of past moments when they said to themselves, "I want to learn to think like an artist," or "I have to master these dances," or "I want to learn to play folk music." They didn't feel pushed by outside forces or compelled to follow a course of action because they "should." They felt a motivation that pulled them from within. They knew what they wanted, and their goals followed naturally.

Often in counseling, when clients tell me that they don't know what they want, I find that they do know what they want—they just don't want to admit it. They think, for reasons that fade under close scrutiny, that they shouldn't want what they want or that they won't be able to get what they want. Maybe they believe they shouldn't want to make money, when that really is what they do want; or maybe they find it shameful to confess that they don't really care about making money. I remember one client reluctantly admitting—as though it were completely unacceptable—that she wanted to live in the country and have a big vegetable garden and be a good nurse and mother! It surprised her to learn that what she wanted sounded perfectly reasonable and possible to me.

Sometimes people reject their goals because they believe that having a goal means they are committed to it forever. But it's okay to change your goals once you've begun. It's okay to go back and reevaluate. You can continue to revise your goals over time, and you may even change them completely. Setting goals and priorities is more of a process than a final decision. You may think you want one thing, but then change your mind once life experience shows you otherwise. It's much better to have goals and change them than to have no goals at all.

Goals are helpful because they set limits and provide constraints. Goals are like the banks of a river, without which the river would lose its momentum and direction. Although limits have a negative connotation, they can fill a positive function. In *The Courage to Create*, Rollo May illustrates the energy-depleting effects of the you-can-do-anything approach: "It's like putting someone into a canoe and pushing him out into the Atlantic toward England with the cheery comment, 'The sky's the limit.'"[42]

Goals should be both directional and flexible. In other words, they need to give you both a sense of direction and more than one way to succeed. An example of a goal that is directional but not flexible is "I want to work for the Royal Shakespeare Company." (What if they don't hire you?) An example of a goal that is flexible but provides no direction is "I want to be rich and famous." (Now what do you do?) You want your goal to give you both a sense of what to do next and the ability to get what you want in more than one way.

For example, when I realized that I didn't want to teach English anymore, I expressed my goals this way: "I want to go into counseling and learn more about psychology." From there I was able to make my goals more clear and specific: "I need to go back to graduate school, and I have different programs in different schools from which to choose." Only then did I learn that there was a field called counseling psychology.

Once you know your career goals, write them down. Begin with the words "I want" and write a complete sentence in the present tense. Try to make your goal statements clear and specific enough that you will know when you have achieved them. Later you can divide your goals into simpler, more manageable sub goals and connect them to taking action closer in time. There is a form for your goal statement in the Career Notebook section of my website (www.creativecareers.com) that you can download and use in your career notebook (described later in this chapter).

If you'd like more help with setting goals, I can recommend a couple of excellent resources. Barbara Sher has written some practical and inspirational self-help manuals for turning dreams into realities. Two of them are *Wishcraft: How to Get What You Really Want*[43] and *I Could Do Anything If I Only Knew What It Was.*[44] She has also developed an audiotape program called Dare to Live Your Dream, which can be ordered via her website at www.barbarasher.com.

MAKE A TIMELINE AND SUBDIVIDE

Once you've set your goals, make a timeline. You need to know not only what you hope to accomplish, but also by when. First decide on the end date, the time by which you hope to have accomplished your goal. Now divide your overall goal into smaller sub goals. Set times by which you hope to have the sub goals accomplished. As you get closer to the next sub goal, divide it into smaller and simpler tasks, so that you know what you hope to accomplish on a monthly, weekly, daily, even hourly basis. The tasks need to be so small that you know you could do them today. Revise your timeline when you get off schedule.

> "If you have built castles in the air, your work need not be lost; that is where they should be. Now put the foundations under them."
>
> —HENRY DAVID THOREAU

Many people find that getting started is the hardest part. By setting simpler sub goals, you make it easier to get started. Once you have accomplished the first step, no matter how short the distance, you'll have greater motivation and energy for the rest of the journey. So learn to set realistic goals that are neither too ambitious nor too easy. You want to feel challenged, not overwhelmed. With practice, you'll get better at setting the right amount of task for the time.

INCREASE YOUR DESIRE FOR YOUR GOAL

It's hard to stay focused on your goals in the midst of living everyday life. The pressure to pay the bills, stop the children from squabbling, get the cat to the vet, and so on can be tremendously distracting. You will help yourself persist if you do some deliberate things to keep your goals in mind. For example, write your goals on the Notes app in your smart phone or on an index card you keep in your shirt pocket. Or tape the card to the refrigerator door or your computer screen, or dangle it from the rearview mirror in your car. Put the card some place where you will see it frequently.

You can consciously choose to make progress toward your goals instead of drifting into what comes naturally at the moment. "Tonight," you can tell yourself, "I am going to put my goals first. I am going to spend the next ten minutes (or one hour or more) writing this cover letter. I am not going to go to the mall or watch TV or visit Facebook." It's like telling yourself that because you want to lose ten pounds by summer, you are not going to eat that bag of M&Ms right now. You put the distant goals before the immediate moment.

You can also consciously strengthen your reasons for attaining your goals. Why do you want to do creative work? Is it because you want to learn new skills, to grow as a person, to make a difference? Do you want to be a good role model for your children? Maybe you want to further your favorite cause in an original way. Choose reasons that are true for you and important to you and tell them to yourself when you want to increase your motivation. Make your creative goals more important through the ways you think about them. Goals that are held with strong commitment are more likely to be realized.

You can also instill hope for yourself through examples of other people who have made their dreams a reality. There are people whose aspirations were similar to your own who have made their dreams come true; you can read their stories and tell yourself, "If they could do it, I can, too." The people in chapter 4 are examples of real people like you and me who have successfully put their talents to work. There are many more. When you read stories about people you admire in newspapers or magazines, cut out the articles and save them. Put them in a notebook like the one described in the next section.

CREATE A CAREER NOTEBOOK

A chef collects favorite recipes; a writer keeps a journal; an artist develops a portfolio. Career adventurers need a place to store and organize their ideas, where they can develop their thinking and keep track of their progress.[45] On my website, creativecareers.com, you will find a framework and set of downloadable support tools for creating a career notebook. This notebook will provide you with a place to record and reflect on your ideas. The support tools are designed to help you choose a career that really suits you. Once you've chosen a career, you can then use your notebook for your job search. And all along, your notebook provides a therapeutic opportunity for self-discovery and personal expression.

The framework is adaptable so you can customize your notebook. For example, you can choose from a scrapbook, a photo album, a three-ring binder, a day planner, a journal, a website, or a smart phone app. You can incorporate drawings, photographs, poetry, handmade paper, sticky notes, envelopes—lots of different creative techniques. Your notebook might include both private and public sections: some parts could remain very personal, while other parts could be shared with helpers in your job search (such as career counselors, librarians, coaches, or people whose work interests you).

The support tools are based on exercises that I developed for my career clients. They are designed to elicit and organize information about your present abilities, interests, and motivators. In fact, as noted in earlier chapters, they include downloadable online versions of the lists of fields, skills, and values in the pages of this book. The exercises will direct you toward a list of occupations to explore.

In addition to the exercises, you might add articles from newspapers and magazines, compliments you've received on your work, drafts of resumes, materials from career workshops, research on various careers, and a list of contacts and resources. Such a notebook can help remind you of your goals and show you how far you've come. To get started, visit the Career Notebook section of my website, www.creativecareers.com.

IDENTIFY YOUR WORK-RELATED VALUES

What do you really want? What values truly motivate you? Only you can say. If I could give my clients just one thing, it would be knowing what they really want. Freely chosen values provide ongoing direction for your life (ongoing because, unlike goals, they are never fully accomplished). Here's a lovely definition of values from Russ Harris, a writer and doctor who trains others to use ACT (Acceptance and Commitment Therapy): "Poetically, they're our heart's deepest desires for how we want to spend our brief time on this planet."[46]

You'll find a list of common work-related values below. You might pick from the following list those values that are most important in your future work. There are no right or wrong choices, only what matters most to you. (Like the other support tools for the career notebook, this list may be downloaded from my website, www.creativecareers.com.)

Many values feel important, so it becomes a matter of which are most important. Some values are independent of each other; other values tend to conflict: higher values for accomplishment tend to result in lower values for a relaxed, low-stress work environment; strong values for service to others tend to lessen the importance of prestige; people who want to do their own thing their own way don't set as much stock on organizational policies and practices.

WORK-RELATED VALUES

Autonomy (I can do the work my own way)

Aesthetics (the work brings more beauty into the world)

Creativity (the work allows me to develop new ideas/products/processes)

Flexible time (work can be arranged outside the traditional workweek)

Prestige (the work gives me respect and a high standing in the eyes of others)

Recognition (others will notice and express admiration for my work)

Economic rewards (my income will be well above the comfort level)

Variety (the work tasks are varied—not routine or monotonous)

Social service and altruism (the work improves the well-being of others)

Challenge (a steep learning curve, so I stay at the growing edge)

Security (I will have steady employment and compensation)

Benefits (the job provides good health care, retirement, and other benefits)

Spiritual (my lifestyle will be consistent with my religious beliefs)

Achievement (a feeling of accomplishment in a job well done)

Personal growth (to continue growing and learning as a person)

Teamwork (my work will be done as part of a team)

Safe environment (fair policies and competent management)

Physically comfortable working environment

Interpersonally harmonious working environment

Opportunity to actualize my potential (develop my strengths by doing what I do best)

Opportunity for advancement

Opportunity to compete and win

Opportunity for adventure

Opportunity to be physically active

Do-it-myself role (I do the work myself)

Influential role (I impact others without having responsibility for their work)

Managerial role (I am in charge, telling others what work to do)

Freelance role (I can take or leave project-based work)

Expert role (I provide information as a knowledge specialist)

As an alternative to this list, or in addition to it, you could take a values test developed by the U. S. Department of Labor. Called the Work Importance Profiler (WIP), it is a computerized assessment that not only identifies your most important values but also connects them to the best matching occupations in the O*NET database. To learn more about the assessment and download it for your use, go to www.onetcenter.org/WIP.html. If you'd prefer to use a values test that is also free and downloadable, but not computerized, then try the Work Importance Locator (WIL) at www.onetcenter.org/WIL.html.

COMMIT CAREFULLY

Some of the best choices you make may be those things you decide against. Expensive cars and executive houses can quickly increase your personal debt and limit your options. In other words, be careful of the commitments you make. That includes nonfinancial commitments, such as your choice of a life partner. In my private practice, I was surprised by how often clients who began with a career problem rather quickly resolved their career issue only to become mired in a deeper and stickier marital issue. A conventional life partner may be extremely threatened by your unconventionality. Some of my clients chose to stifle their creativity rather than to rock the boat in their marriage. On the other hand, some stayed true to themselves and found that their partners moved from fearing their creativity to enjoying the excitement they brought to the marriage.

RESIST PERFECTIONISM

In part, perfectionism is inherent in the nature of the creative task. The process of reaching for an ideal and bringing your ideas to excellence requires perfectionist tendencies and, at the same time, engenders frustration, because making mistakes is also built into the creative process. But sometimes the hunger for perfection is so powerful that we become passive, because only by doing nothing can we avoid the possibility of making an error. Then, unfortunately, we also stop learning and growing.

In literature, greatness is not equal to perfection. *Hamlet* and *Huckleberry Finn*, for example, are universally agreed to be great works of fiction—and yet volumes have been written about their flaws and imperfections. If you want to make a great contribution, your work doesn't need to be perfect, and neither do you. It's a good thing, too, because the concept of perfection doesn't apply to human nature. It's like applying the concept of nobility to a rutabaga.

"Failures and successes are intimate relatives; if you want to dine with the latter, you must occasionally sit down with the former, especially as you sometimes can't tell them apart until about the third course."

—DAVID CAMPBELL

"The books I haven't written are better than the books other people have."

—CYRIL CONNOLLY

Unfortunately, perfectionism results from a naturally occurring developmental phenomenon: our critical abilities develop more quickly than our productive abilities. It is the rare and very fortunate young person whose creative abilities are recognized early and nurtured to the point that the person's artistic skills can withstand his or her own quickly developing critical appraisal. So many people who ask me for help begin by telling me that they fear they don't have the talent they need, and I respond by saying that they probably didn't have the opportunity to develop their talent before they became too critical for their own good. Try leaning into your growing edge, rather than attacking it as a kamikaze critic. Risk failure, and then be gentle with yourself.

If perfectionism is a problem for you, consult the chapter titled "Dare to Be Average" in David Burns's best-selling, straight-thinking book, *Feeling Good.* Let me quote from the last paragraph in that chapter:

> "In fact, just think what it would be like if you were perfect. There'd be nothing to learn, no way to improve, and life would be completely void of challenge and the satisfaction that comes from mastering something that takes effort. It would be like going to kindergarten for the rest of your life. You'd know all the answers and win every game. Every project would be a guaranteed success because you would do everything correctly. People's conversations would offer you nothing because you'd already know it all. And most important, nobody could love or relate to you. It would be impossible to feel any love for someone who was flawless and knew it all."[47]

LEARN TO VALIDATE YOURSELF

In general, people who take a conventional approach get approval from others as a matter of course. One of the best conventional things I ever did was to have a baby, and I enjoyed all the positive attention and approval I received during pregnancy and early motherhood. On the other hand, people who take an unconventional approach are likely to meet with disapproval or total disinterest. When I was beginning to think about writing this book, for example, most people were simply not interested. If I had needed people to respond to my writing goals the way they responded to the baby, you would not now be reading this book.

In fact, most people will not be able to see and appreciate your vision until you realize it more fully and bring it into existence for them, and that takes some time. If your creative work has not yet brought you approval, try patting your own back. Tell yourself what a good idea it is and how well you are doing. Remind yourself that you're a swan, not an ugly duckling. When people ask you what you do, say, "I'm a cartoonist," or "I'm working on creative solutions to the problem of overpopulation." Define yourself by something you feel good about. Don't define yourself exclusively by your day-job title, especially if it's one that makes you feel apologetic.

Money is such a clear way to demonstrate success, a universal yardstick for measuring personal worth. A high income brings instant respect. But in an already affluent society in which spending money has become the national pastime, striving to make even more money takes a huge toll. Stress is at an all-time high. Fortunately, there seems to be a growing cultural trend away from materialism. People are opting for quality of life over quantity of possessions as they realize what really makes people happy: not a super high income, but good interpersonal relationships and meaningful work.

Learn to validate yourself with regard to your income. If you haven't done so already, think about what success means to you. Once you have independently defined it, it will bother you less if you are not "successful" by yesterday's conventional standards.

Don't measure yourself against an obsolete model of career advancement, either. How many people do you know whose career progress looks like the trail of a rocket?

How many have even climbed the proverbial career ladder? Various authors have had some fun with the now old-fashioned metaphor of the career ladder. Cliff Hakim has replaced it with a career lattice, to indicate the possibility of sideways movement. Peter Drucker said, "The stepladder is gone, and there's not even the implied structure of an industry's rope ladder. It's more like vines, and you bring your own machete."

Once you are past basic security needs, happiness seems to be more about doing than having, anyway. What I do with my time forty hours a week feels more important to me than what kind of a car I drive. When I asked some conventionally successful people what they wanted for their children, they did not say, "I want them to have a six-figure salary and an estate like mine." On the contrary, they said they wanted their children to work at something important to them to which they had to give their all. The people who were successful enough to appear in the 1996 *Who's Who in America* were asked how they defined success. According to a Yankelovich poll reported in *USA Today,* few in the group defined success as having money or power, but many mentioned doing work you love, having a loving family, and making a lasting contribution to your field.[48]

> "Sad to say, the road to good intentions is paved with hell."
>
> —**LEE ROY BEACH**

ANTICIPATE DIFFICULTY

When you choose a challenging, nonlinear path, you can expect times when you feel down and times when the work is not going well. You'll find barriers in your path because that's life and that's the nature of an adventure, not because there is something wrong with you. Anticipating difficulties makes them easier to bear. In fact, you might even consider planning for difficulties and setbacks.

When people try to change their habits, they often fail. That's human and to be expected: we all make mistakes. However, people get in trouble when they interpret a single mistake as a total failure and then abandon all further effort. The classic dieting example is the dieter who eats one doughnut—and then feels so bad about going off her diet that she eats a full dozen! Instead, we can turn our mistakes into opportunities for learning.

Let's apply this idea to the job search. Suppose that to pursue your creative goals you need to talk to an important person in your field. But you don't, because you feel too shy. To keep the lapse (not calling once) from becoming a relapse (never calling at all), have a plan worked out ahead of time for how you will respond when your actions don't reflect your good intentions. Maybe, for example, you could start by contacting someone less intimidating or writing down what you want to say and practicing with a friend. Commit yourself to getting back on track as soon as possible after a failure, and then congratulate yourself for having done it. When it comes to changing habits, the more you try, the better your chances for success.

ASK FOR HELP

Everyone—even self-sufficient creative types—can benefit from the help provided by other people. The stresses of life are easier to bear when we have supportive people to share our joys and sorrows and to offer practical assistance. When we are socially connected through our work and other social contexts, we function more effectively.

Most people get social approval from behaving conventionally. Every college student knows that having a safe, recognizable major that is presumed to lead to gainful employment will elicit approving comments from parents and friends. If you choose an unconventional path, though, you may need to be more deliberate about garnering support. Remember that relationships work best when they meet mutual needs: you will get support, but you will also give it.

Sometimes creative people fail to nurture the supportive relationships that are available to them. They deny their need for help and bend over backward to be independent, and their interpersonal needs go underground in fantasies of fame and fortune. But acclaim from afar is not the same as helpful relationships in real life. Worse yet, acclaim based on achievement is conditional. A star college quarterback once wryly commented that he was only as popular as his last pass. Furthermore, celebrity status offers no buffer to the stresses of everyday life. As a glance at any tabloid will tell you, the rich and famous are as vulnerable as the rest of us to divorce, depression, drug abuse, and disease.

At the Academy Awards, the winners thank their mentors, family, and friends. They are the first to say they didn't do it alone. You don't have to do it alone, either. You can ask for help.

FIND SOMEONE WHO BELIEVES IN YOUR ABILITY TO CREATE

Creative people need at least one supportive person who believes in their ability to create. That person could be your parent, your spouse, your therapist, your friend . . . it really doesn't matter, as long as they are there for you and believe in you. Their faith in your ability will make the stresses of the creative role easier to bear. You can't make this kind of relationship happen, but you can nurture it when it comes along.

The Artist's Way: A Spiritual Path to Higher Creativity by Julia Cameron is a do-it-yourself guide for recovering from artist's block. The twelve-week program to free your creativity includes weekly self-nurturing "dates" with your inner creative child. Cameron claims, "I have seen blocked painters paint, broken poets speak in tongues, halt and lame and maimed writers racing through final drafts. . . . it is not too late or too egotistical or too selfish or too silly to work on your creativity."[49]

LEARN TO WORK WITH A CRITIC

It's surprisingly hard to get candid, objective criticism. Many people are not critical, either because they are afraid of damaging the relationship or because they aren't able to think critically. A good critic can help you in ways that you can't help yourself. Their objective feedback can help you improve your creative work without doing harm to your self-esteem. Find someone who is willing and able to give you the kind of feedback you need and then nurture that relationship.

One of my hobbies is decorating my own home. I have a vision of how I want things to look, and I enjoy selecting and arranging colors and shapes and textures to create that effect. To help me achieve my goals, I have developed a relationship with an interior designer who functions as a critic. She has more experience and more knowledge than I do, and she can provide feedback on my ideas and suggest alternatives. I trust her to help me make aesthetic choices that make the most of my budget.

It doesn't have to be a single critic, either. Feedback from many sources can be even more valuable. Eager for feedback, cartoonist Scott Adams put his email address alongside his comic strip. He quickly learned that the business-oriented strips were the most popular. He switched his emphasis to business to give his readers what they wanted, and that was when *Dilbert* took off.

DEVELOP A RELATIONSHIP WITH A MENTOR

Mentors are people whose work you admire, individuals who are further along on your chosen career path and thus able to offer both wisdom and practical guidance. Their vision and encouragement can enlarge your sense of the possibilities. Mentors are often real people that you know, such as teachers or experts or leaders in your field.

If you don't yet have a relationship with a real-life mentor, you can use your imagination to develop a relationship with a symbolic mentor. One experimental psychologist claimed as her mentor a renowned woman psychologist she never knew personally but whose research she admired. One of my clients, a writer and diarist, told me that she found a mentor in that great character of children's fiction, Harriet the Spy. When others read her diary, my client remembered how Harriet had survived a similar misfortune. You could also read biographies and autobiographies. Learning how creators you admire overcame obstacles equal to your own may give you strength.

JOIN A SUPPORT GROUP

"Isolation is the dream killer," says team-builder Barbara Sher. If you feel alone in your struggle to create an unconventional niche for yourself, find a group of people in the same boat. Look for people who share your values, people who can offer emotional support and benefit from your support as well. A group of like-minded people can provide the approval and assistance you don't receive from the conventional world. One example of such a group would be A.R.T.S. Anonymous, a twelve-step group open to those who want to express their creativity (www.artsanonymous.org).

Meetups are gatherings of people based around a particular interest or activity, like art, music, photography, and so forth. These meetings are run and organized either by experts or by ordinary people who are passionate about their interest area. For examples, bloggers use meetups to improve their WordPress skills. Meetups are a terrific way to get together with people in your chosen field, where you can see if you will be a good fit and learn how to break in. Using the Meetup website (www.meetup.com), search in your area by field of interest. Some Meetups are geared more toward hobbyists and others more toward professionals. If you don't see a Meetup related to your interests, you might start your own.

A formal support group offered by a social agency or an educational institution is another possibility, but so is an informal network of peers, people who you bring together by calling them and arranging to meet for lunch. You can also decrease your isolation by staying connected with groups in your field: read newsletters and trade journals, go to conferences, participate in your local chapter or national association, join an online discussion group, and attend special events. For example, ceramicists enjoy a special event when they fire a kiln as a group. Everyone places their pieces in the kiln, and then all members take turns stoking the fire.

Many job seekers focus on what they lack, fearing that they are the only ones who may not be skilled enough or educated enough or young enough or financially cushioned enough. In a job-hunting support group, you'll quickly learn that you are not alone! Your career counselor, local librarian, or Workforce Center should be able to help you find support groups in your community.

MAKE A CONTRACT WITH OTHERS

If you tell others what you hope to accomplish and make a contract with them, you'll be more likely to achieve your goals than if you simply make a promise to yourself. Weight Watchers uses this principle when they have dieters weigh in at meetings. Find a person or a group to whom you can report and set up a regular meeting time. State your goals publicly. Tell others what you expect to do in the coming week and ask them to check your progress the following week. This is more fun if they also are working toward a goal and can check in with you. Then attend those meetings religiously!

TAKE ADVANTAGE OF PUBLIC SUPPORT

Crowdfunding has become a viable means of garnering public funds for personal projects. Kickstarter is a web-based international crowdfunding platform that is devoted specifically to bringing creative projects to fruition. In the last five years, they've gathered more than one billion dollars in pledges from millions of backers to support more than 65,000 creative projects. Yours could be next! To learn more, visit www.kickstarter.com.

In addition, traditional government social service agencies exist to support creative endeavors. In the United Kingdom, the national organizations are called Arts Council England (www.artscouncil.org.uk), the Arts Council of Wales (www.artswales.org.uk), and the Scottish Arts Council (www.creativescotland.com). In Ireland, contact the Irish Arts Council (www.artscouncil.ie). In Canada, the national organization is called Canada Council for the Arts (www.canadacouncil.ca). In Australia, it's the Australia Council for the Arts (www.australiacouncil.gov.au). In New Zealand, it's the Creative NZ–Arts Council of New Zealand (www.creativenz.govt.nz). Each of these organizations offers grants and other forms of support for creative endeavors.

If you live in the United States, contact your state arts council. It will be in the phone book or on the website with other state agencies, with a name something like Commission on Arts, Council on the Arts, or Arts Board. Some state arts funds come from the National Endowment for the Arts, which provides financial assistance in the form of fellowships, grants, and studio space. These funds are released to institutions, groups, and individuals. You can register with your state agency to receive information on new opportunities.

Some state arts councils sponsor artist-in-residence programs. Public schools, art schools, university art departments, and other organizations offer short-term residencies to artists and other creators. Your state arts council can also give you information on the Art in Public Places program, which is funded by the General Services Administration (GSA). The GSA is permitted to spend a small percentage of federal construction monies on art. Your librarian can help you locate more information on public support. Ask to see a foundation directory. It lists foundations that support the arts, such as the Guggenheim, Rockefeller, and Ford foundations.

On a state or county level in the United States, you can receive free career services through your local Workforce Center or CareerOneStop Center. These agencies are not devoted specifically to creative jobs, but they do offer a number of practical services, such as information, Internet access, workshops, jobs fairs, and job postings. You can find the location of the closest center to your home online at www.careeronestop.org.

The Actors' Fund is a national organization serving entertainers and performing artists. They provide a range of social services, including employment, housing, and health programs. They have offices in New York City, Chicago, and Los Angeles. The headquarters phone number is (212) 221-7300 and their website is www.actorsfund.org.

MAKE THE MOST OF SOCIAL MEDIA

Since the previous edition of this book was published, using social media has become another important career strategy for providing a powerful way to build community and stay connected. The most well-known social networking platforms are LinkedIn, Facebook, and Twitter. Google+ (or Google Plus) offers some unique features and seems to be steadily gaining traction. Beyond these staples, there are hosts (no pun intended) of other networking sites dedicated to fostering creative community. Pinterest, Etsy, Behance, and DeviantART are just a few that come to mind.

You may already be a social media junkie with a strong online presence and a long list of connections and followers. Or you may think of social media as a big waste of time and energy. A focus on social media may cause some of you to want to toss this book aside. Many artists say that they would rather spend time *being* creative than posting and tweeting about art. In the name of adventure, I encourage you to keep an open mind.

Many recruitment and job search experts claim that a mere 20 percent of all jobs ever get posted. In other words, a whopping 80 percent of positions are filled through referrals or some form of networking. "Who you know" is more important than ever in terms of learning about and landing opportunities. Whether you are looking for a paid position, a freelance gig, or a way to collaborate, your connections can become your allies, helping you along the path to achieving your career goals.

LINKEDIN

Many people think that LinkedIn is strictly for business professionals seeking conventional jobs. Think again. You are just as likely to find a graphic designer, freelance photojournalist, or video game developer on LinkedIn as you are an accountant, a pharmaceutical sales rep, or a manager of human resources. LinkedIn currently boasts 300 million members in more than 200 countries. That includes professionals and opportunities from across all industries, including Fortune 500 companies, arts organizations, nonprofits, government agencies, institutions of higher learning, and small businesses. Freelancers and independent contractors are prominent.

Still feeling doubtful? You need to know that potential employers, clients, and new contacts quite often conduct an online search to learn about you before making an offer, partnering on a project, or even meeting for coffee. Having a LinkedIn profile used to be merely a good idea—but now there is almost a sense that something is wrong if you don't have a profile set up. In other words, not being "found" on LinkedIn can work against you. A strong LinkedIn profile helps build connections and credibility.

One of the best things about LinkedIn is that you can customize your profile to convey your personal brand. Yes, you really do need to start thinking of yourself as a brand! Some people shudder at the thought; however, your personal brand is what sets you apart from others who share similar interests, talents, and skills. It is a projection of how you see yourself and how you hope others will perceive you. So, ask yourself: "What do I want people to think of when they view my profile or when they come across a discussion posting with my name on it? What are the general qualities or areas of expertise I want associated with my brand?" Without a clear, compelling brand it is far too easy to disappear into cyberspace.

Building a strong online profile offers a perfect opportunity to tap into your creative talents. Your picture, headline, and professional summary, as well as the groups you join and the organizations you "follow" all work together to paint a picture of who you are, what you do, and the particular causes that matter most to you. You can add hyperlinks to your personal website, blog, or portfolio. You can even upload a video of yourself teaching a workshop, blowing glass, or arranging flowers. You need not spend a lot of money creating a professional video. Raw film clips shot with your smart phone can be equally as appealing. Your LinkedIn profile should be professional, but that does not mean it needs to be sterile or dull. The goal is to create an authentic introduction of you and your work.

FACEBOOK

Facebook is more than a way to share quick updates with family and friends: you can use Facebook both personally *and* professionally. On Facebook, you can actually keep these two parts of your life fairly separate.

Within your personal account, Facebook allows you to create or join groups made up of select friends who share similar interests and passions. This is a great way for freelancers or artists to promote themselves and build a following. You can also set up a more formal business page that is completely separate from your personal account. A Facebook for Business division has been introduced to help sole proprietors and small businesses garner new customers and increase sales. As of this writing, there are 30 million active small business pages on Facebook.

Keep in mind that it takes time to set up and administer a Facebook business page. Online courses and tutorials will help you get started, but the process can be a bit complex, and there are fees involved.

Nevertheless, many creative professionals report positive results from having a Facebook business page. It can be a fairly low-cost way to enhance your brand, link traffic back to your blog or website, and expand your customer base. Whether you decide to keep it personal or create a more formal business presence on Facebook, you want to be sure that you are always presenting the very best image of yourself to the world.

TWITTER

If you do an online search for the best social media sites for artists, you will likely find Twitter on the top of the list. Along with more conventional workers, this is where musicians, photographers, painters, sculptors, actors, dancers, writers, comedians, and many of the world's most creative thinkers gather. Spending time on Twitter can get your imaginative juices flowing and reassure you that the artistic spirit is alive and well in the world!

Twitter now boasts some 255 million monthly members and sends an astounding 500 million tweets per day. It has become a creative hub for making valuable connections, developing friendships, and engaging more intimately with a particular audience. Many companies now use Twitter as part of their overall recruitment strategy to source and hire top talent. With the right presence on Twitter, you may find yourself being courted by a recruiter or a new creative partner.

GOOGLE+ (GOOGLE PLUS)

While Google+ cannot currently boast an enormous membership, many predict that it will soon become the next big thing in terms of online community. Social media experts cite three reasons for this. First, the platform is clean, simple, and user-friendly. Second, it is easy to meet new people on Google+, and the format tends to encourage longer conversations and deeper relationships. Finally, the "circles" feature allows you to build community with people who share your specific passions and interests. For instance, you can create a circle of "Writers and Journalists," allowing you an easy way to follow news and participate in discussions specifically related to writing and journalism.

On LinkedIn and Facebook, you generally need to wade through a lot of noise to find posts that are of interest, because LinkedIn and Facebook group us by who we know across all industries and areas of interest. Google+, on the other hand, offers a unique combination of "circles" and "hangouts" to help you connect with people who share your specific interests and passions.

I am not suggesting that you get involved in all of these different platforms. Social media is not meant to replace your local community. You might set a goal to explore one new online network. Do some research, test the waters, and take small steps. As you put one foot in front of the other, continue to scan the horizon. The social media landscape is constantly shifting; some established sites go away while new ones emerge. You will eventually find a community or two that aligns with your style and supports your needs and goals.

Regardless of which social platforms you join, keep your presence fresh and productive. First, you want to make sure that the image you project is professional and positive. Sloppy and incomplete profiles or negative posts are not going to attract the attention you want. Second, commit to being an active member in the communities you join. For example, it is not enough to simply have a LinkedIn account. The goal is to participate in discussions, post articles of interest, and keep your profile up-to-date. Finally, look for opportunities to be generous and helpful. Social media does not have to be a narcissistic, self-indulgent pastime. Congratulate your connections on their successes, recommend others for their unique talents, publicize a colleague's event within your network, and generously share ideas and information.

STILL STRUGGLING TO MOVE FORWARD?

Even if it seems like none of these strategies will work for you, adopt a trial-and-error approach. Try them all. Some will work better than others. Adapt those that work somewhat so they work even better, and then spend more of your time on the strategies that are best for you. Remember, too, that your behavior does not depend on your emotional state. You can feel unhappy, miserable, negative, and scared, and still take steps that will move you closer to your goals. In fact, taking action can have a *positive effect* on your feelings!

If you have tried different ways to use your head and ask for help, but you are stuck and can't seem to move forward, you probably need to focus less on your conscious intentions and attend more to the context in which you are acting. It's like the shift from figure to ground in those optical illusions in which if you look at it one way, it's the profile of two women, and if you look the other way, it's a vase. So let's shift now to the ground on which you take action.

FIGHT YOUR FEARS

Most of us fear change even when we consciously want change. Grossly underrated by the common person in the street, fear is our most typical block, a very frequent and normal human emotion. Creativity researchers have found that many people are even afraid of their creativity! When they are first asked to be creative, subjects in creativity experiments often express fear that their creations will be "too wild or bizarre."[50] However, once they get started and gain some experience as a creator, they tend to become more comfortable with and even excited by creative activities. If you feel yourself blocked from doing something you want to do, try asking yourself, "What is the worst that can happen?"

In situations that make you feel anxious, try taking small, well-planned steps to get around the obstacles or fears blocking your path. As you gain

> "Whatever you think you can do or believe you can do, begin it. Action has magic, grace, and power in it."
>
> **—JOHANN WOLFGANG VON GOETHE**

> "Fear stops action. Action cures fear."
>
> **—MARGARET BOURKE-WHITE**

experience and confidence, you'll be able to take larger steps and bolder risks. For example, a poet might start writing only for him- or herself, then progress to sharing a single poem with a trusted friend, then asking for feedback on a work in progress from a small writer's group, and so on, before finally performing in public. (One woman took this a step further—after following all these steps, she then booked her first reading without telling her friends or family. That way, she figured, if she was a failure, no one she cared about would know. When the evening went well, she felt comfortable inviting everyone she knew to her second reading.)

GET PROFESSIONAL HELP

Therapists are professionals who can help you in many different ways. They may see what you can't see. If you think you are doing everything right but something's clearly not working, it may be that (as is true for everyone) there are parts of yourself you can't see. Self-help books can help you with the conscious tasks of advancing your career, but they won't help you become aware of the unconscious ways you contribute to problems. And if you are not aware, there is nothing you can do.

I've worked with many people who were clinically depressed but didn't think they were depressed because they did not feel sad. Instead, they felt empty or numb and very tired. Although pep talks and appeals to their willpower couldn't snap them out of it, a therapeutic relationship and an antidepressant helped them get back on track. If you are not moving forward with your career because you are too tired to move anywhere, you may need treatment for depression as a first step. Other reasons for seeking counseling include uncomfortable levels of anxiety, fear of commitment, lack of confidence, and conflicts with significant others over your career plans.

Many therapists are relationship experts. If you have trouble maintaining relationships that nurture and support you, therapy can help you with that. A therapist can teach good interpersonal skills through modeling, role-playing, and feedback. If you currently lack the support you need, a therapist can substitute for your support network and fill the roles of mentor, external monitor, and person-who-believes-in-your-ability-to-create. A therapist can also help you locate support groups and other community resources.

The best way to find a therapist is by personal referral. Kooks and flakes seem to be overrepresented in the ranks of therapists, and as a buyer you need to beware. As a result of counseling, you should feel empowered. If you don't feel empowered or don't trust your therapist, talk to him or her about it, and if the problem doesn't clear up, leave. Whether you choose a career counselor, clinical social worker, licensed psychologist, or even a psychiatrist, the person's credentials are less important than the quality of relationship between the two of you. There are competent and not-so-competent helpers in all fields.

If you don't have a personal referral and aren't sure where to start, I recommend searching for an ACT therapist. Acceptance and Commitment Therapy (ACT) is part of the positive psychology movement, and I'm impressed by its background principles. The founders of ACT believe that it's easy for the problem-solving tendencies of the human mind to take over, leading us into a grim and relentless focus on solving problems. Therapy will help you gain flexibility and courage, so you're able to live your life more like it's an adventure.

DON'T ABUSE DRUGS AND ALCOHOL

History is filled with romantic, rebellious images of artists as drunks and drug users—and, indeed, creative and unconventional people often seem to be drawn to substance abuse. Perhaps it has to do with this mystique, or with the notion that rules and guidelines are for other, more conventional people. Just be aware, however, that no matter how much of a free spirit you are, you aren't likely to move forward in life if your brain is awash in alcohol or other drugs.

People who use substances tend to move backward, rather than forward, as their substance abuse creates new problems to compound the ones they are avoiding through intoxication. Drug and alcohol abuse creates problems such as accidents, loss of jobs or relationships, and a greater likelihood of crime and family violence. You know you are dependent when you need more drugs or alcohol to get the same effects and if you experience withdrawal when you don't use them.

Even if you have the I.Q. of a genius, you can't expect your brain to function up to its potential if it's swimming in a sea of toxic substances. If you have been abusing substances, try the suggestions in this chapter after you stop. You'll get better results. If you find that you aren't able to maintain reasonable limits, seek professional help or join a self-help group such as Alcoholics Anonymous.

PRACTICE MINDFULNESS

To my way of thinking, mindfulness meditation is the mental health equivalent of flossing your teeth. Mindfulness is about learning how to stay present and pay attention to how we actually think and feel and behave, which allows us to respond more positively and effectively to life's challenges. There are many benefits to mindfulness practice, including decreased stress and increased resilience. Some people fear that meditation carries with it a set of religious beliefs. Not so. Mindfulness can be practiced without adding Buddhist or other religious beliefs. I recommend beginning with an introductory class. You'll also find many self-help books on the subject.

GIVE YOURSELF TIME

If your destination is clear and you are taking the necessary steps, but you don't feel like you are getting closer to your goals, you may not have given yourself enough time. After all, this whole chapter has been about delayed gratification. Delayed gratification—what's that again? I have to confess that I have found it much easier to tell my clients to be patient with their process than to be patient with my own! Perhaps we've seen too many cheesy dramatizations that gloss over the background effort that goes into an achievement, instead focusing on the cheering crowd that greets the result.

Doing something new takes time. If you are starting a personal business venture, it is unlikely to be an overnight success, and if you are too impatient for signs of success, you may inaccurately assume something is wrong and give up prematurely. Even after you have devoted your time and other resources to getting a new product or service ready for the market, you can still expect it to take a while to catch on. New products and services usually take as much time to go from 0 to 10 percent of the market as they do to go from 10 to 90 percent.

> "No great thing is created suddenly, any more than a bunch of grapes or a fig. If you tell me that you desire a fig, I answer you that there must be time. Let it first blossom, then bear fruit, then ripen."
>
> —EPICTETUS

If your aspirations are to greatness, you will probably need to give yourself many years before you see big results. Mozart didn't complete a masterpiece until about ten years after he began composing. Working together as already established artists, it took Braque and Picasso eight years to develop Cubism. And those time frames are not unusual. Benjamin Bloom, a psychologist and researcher, found that people who had achieved world-class status in their respective fields had spent at least ten years during which they had "devoted more time, energy, and thought to their talent areas than to any other activity or area of their lives."[51]

Those ten years may not include the time it takes for the public to appreciate what you have done: the general public was not aware of the Wright brothers' achievement until five years after they had invented the world's first airplane! Lincoln's Gettysburg Address was poorly received in 1863, and he felt it had been a failure. He had no idea that his short speech would go down in American history. The architect Eiffel was ridiculed for the Eiffel Tower, now the symbol of Paris. Critics in 1888 compared his structure to a factory chimney, a monster, and a skeleton.

Since gratification in the form of public recognition may be a long time in coming, it's important to find ways to reinforce yourself all along. A life of rigorous discipline can be unnecessarily bleak and even counterproductive. Take some breaks. Find little ways to reward yourself every day. You might schedule something you enjoy—such as watching a movie or getting a massage—after a block of time devoted to your career goals. And when something goes really well for you, celebrate! Invite your helpers and supporters to celebrate with you.

You may feel at this point that creating an unconventional niche for yourself is way more effort than you bargained for. I can't blame you. I can't tell you the number of times I've wished it was easier myself. But don't let a few hardships along the way discourage you. They are an inevitable part—but only one part—of your adventure. Today's setback may become tomorrow's blessing in disguise. Eventually, you'll create a lifestyle that sustains your creativity, enabling you to spend years of your life doing something you love. Besides, right now, in the short term, the joy of the creative process is yours. You can experience that today!

Chapter 6
THE PROCESS OF YOUR ADVENTURE

By now you have probably figured out a way to make your unconventionality an advantage in our changing work world. Maybe you know how you want to support yourself, and you've chosen your best strategies for making your dreams come true. But if you are like most people, you may find that instead of taking action, you are gazing at your navel, slightly paralyzed by the uncertainties ahead. You need to call on your courage, and that might be easier if you had an idea of what to expect.

What lies ahead of you? An adventure that is both tough and fun. As you pursue your unconventional career goals, you become a hero on a journey—meeting challenges, suffering through adversity, and growing as a person. My friend Laurel Gray, a choreographer who specializes in Central Asian and Silk Road dance culture and who founded and directs her own dance company, compared her journey to Dorothy's in *The Wizard of Oz*. On the way to creating her career, Laurel traveled to exotic places she'd never been before, like Oz; she found friends and supporters like the Tin Man and the Scarecrow; and she also suffered at the hands of rivals who were green with envy, like the Wicked Witch of the West.

The journey has long been a popular metaphor, helping us to recognize that sometimes there is greater joy in traveling than in reaching the destination. What an exciting adventure you enjoyed along the way! What an amazing person you have become! So it is with your creative career.

The development of your creativity is a lifelong unfolding of the self as you change and grow over time. Let's take a closer look at the process as it may unfold in your own life.

Changes often begin with an ending. In other words, before you can be reborn to something new, something old must die. In *Transitions: Making Sense of Life's Changes*, author William Bridges pays homage to the mythic "death and rebirth" quality of life transition.[52] The death may be symbolic, in the sense that what you have lost was only an illusion about how the work world ought to be. Or maybe your sense of self has changed enough that your old job no longer fits the person you have become.

Not all endings are symbolic. Many careers end unexpectedly these days, as more workers are laid off, downsized, or fired, often without warning. Some people quit, fed up with being harassed in the workplace. Some become so stressed out that they physically can't work any longer. Some endings are happy—as, for example, when people graduate or successfully finish a major project. Whether you have lost your job, or graduated from college, or given up on pleasing your parents, an ending ushers in a new beginning.

Let's explore what happens next. As you become the hero of your own life's adventure, you follow a process with some predictable stages. I'll name these stages "opening to the call," "committing to the call," "fulfilling the call," and "returning with a gift."

OPENING TO THE CALL

After an ending, you may feel like you're living in limbo or no-man's-land. In this place of emptiness and confusion, you aren't sure what you want. Reality looks different, compared to how it looked before. You may feel like you are going crazy. It's uncomfortable, perhaps even almost unbearable at times. You instinctively withdraw, taking a time-out from the conventional world. Bridges says, "It is into some rabbit hole or cave or forest wilderness that creative individuals have always withdrawn on the eve of their rebirth."[53]

Don't try to escape; don't try to force the process; don't expect to feel good. You will be uncomfortable. Endure. Forget about efficiency. Your creativity will benefit from not being so busy for a while anyway. As far as I am concerned, conventional productivity is overrated. Our extreme busyness tends to interfere with the creative process. How can good ideas take root when we are way too frenetic to muse and catch the odd connection? The important thing now is to keep yourself open to new possibilities.

This is a good time to think about what you learned in the recently ended phase of life, to look for advantages and disadvantages to the change, and to express some of your feelings and ideas. Paint; write in a journal; play your instrument; talk things over with a counselor or confidante; begin your career notebook. Get a temporary structure in place, something that supports you (such as a free place to live or an interim job) during your open but empty time.

> "We make a living by what we get, but we make a life by what we give."
>
> —WINSTON CHURCHILL

At the beginning of a creative career, just as at the beginning of a creative project, you may not be able to say exactly what you are doing or how

> "Man matures through work which inspires him to difficult good."
>
> —POPE JOHN PAUL II

you are going to proceed. The problem itself is not clear. Clients of mine who struggle with this ambiguity tell me that they wish their goals were clearer and that they could move more quickly along a straighter path. They wish they felt more secure. They feel distressed and anxious, as if something must be "wrong"—yet from my perspective their feelings are appropriate and understandable.

Submitting yourself to the creative process is like falling in love. You feel shaky and uncertain on the inside, especially at the beginning. Joy and transformation await, but first you must take a risk and make yourself vulnerable—and that's scary. There is a natural desire to stay safe and secure, to not face the unknown. But if you play it safe, staying within conventional boundaries, you miss out on the romance of your own life's adventure. So, come on! Listen to that small voice inside.

Creativity is an equal-opportunity adventure. It doesn't matter whether you are a neophyte or already a superstar. You could be just beginning your career, or already well established, or retired. You could reside in a palace or a prison. You could have been born with a silver spoon in your mouth or have survived a dysfunctional family from hell. You could be a member of the majority or minority group in any country in the world. And you are never too young or too old: Claude Monet didn't even start his water lily series until he was in his seventies; Goethe finished *Faust* in his eighties; Pablo Casals was still performing in his nineties.

COMMITTING TO THE CALL

Do you hear a call? Maybe you have heard multiple small calls and allowed them to nudge you. You feel intimations, subtle attractions, small moments in which you begin to imagine a new future, one in which your purpose and meaning take larger shape. You nurture new ideas, giving them a safe harbor. It isn't glamorous or impressive, but it is a beginning. Often, the ideas come to you from an unexpected source.

The artist in your soul may awaken when you encounter the work of a master. You resonate to it, although you may not recognize its importance at the time. I was once part of an audience who had gathered to question a panel of Northwest comedians about how they became successful in their careers. As the comedians answered questions and listened to each other, it dawned on them that they all began their careers as children, when they were inspired by listening to their favorite comedians on the radio. When they were kids, they did not realize they would eventually become comedians. But later they pointed to those moments as the beginning of their identity.

Your gifts may also be awakened by situations that seem mysterious or obviously wrong to you. We usually speak of people finding a problem, but one of my sculptor clients said that the problems always seemed to find her. Maybe you are motivated by an important social need or excited by a revolutionary idea. Many feminists from different disciplines became engaged in creative action because of problems related to gender. Roseanne Barr, for example, has said that her drive to do standup comedy grew out of her frustration with the way she was treated as a housewife and mother.

> "If you can see the path laid out in front of you, step by step—it's not your path!"
>
> —JOSEPH CAMPBELL

The most important action you can take at the beginning of your journey is to accept your gifts and the difficulties they bring with them. Sometimes gifted people deny their talent because they fear that doing creative work will prevent them from getting something else they want, such as security or prestige. But

> "Works of art are indeed always products of having been in danger, of having gone to the very end in an experience, to where man can go no further."
>
> —RAINER MARIA RILKE

although denial and avoidance may work in the short run, they simply won't work in the long run. Something of the irresistibility of your gifts is implied by the words *vocation* and *occupation*. Vocation is defined as a calling; occupation means to take possession of, to seize.

If we believe data from the Johnson O'Connor Research Foundation, an organization that began testing human aptitudes in 1922, it appears that you can't ignore your talents, because they won't ignore you. Johnson

O'Connor researchers found that people who ignored their gifts in their career and life planning were frustrated and unhappy by midlife, and they urged that you use your talents either in your job or in your hobbies. As the ancient Greek playwrights implied, you can't avoid your fate. In fact, it makes more sense to try embracing your gifts and accepting the career challenges they present to you.

Theologian Matthew Fox shares the experience of one of his students who had both affirmed and rejected her creative gifts:

> *"When I have been attentive to the creative gifts within, I have been free to play and grow as a human being. When I have cooperated in the denial of those gifts, or when I have chosen to set them aside I have withered. My love of life has suffered. I have stopped praying, I have become small and cynical, or I have driven myself to the point of exhaustion and burnout. I have become a compulsive worker trying to make up in my work what I have denied in my most creative self."*[54]

A career adventure will almost certainly require sacrifice. People with the most exciting and glamorous careers usually make some sacrifices in their personal lives. Maybe they delay getting married or never have kids. People who do intrinsically satisfying creative work often make less money than their more extrinsically motivated conventional counterparts. You, too, may have to let go of something precious to you, such as a romantic self-image. Or financial security. Or social status. Or pleasing your spouse. Or enjoying a creative lifestyle until you work out a way to support yourself. Something you value will be sacrificed for an even greater good.

Some people don't want to plant seeds unless they are confident that those seeds will flourish and become prize-winning plants. They are scared to commit unless they are sure they have the talent to make it big. If you love something and are willing to work hard, don't prematurely conclude that you haven't got what it takes. Your talent is a potential in you. Your early work is not necessarily an indicator of where you can go.

Many great creators were late bloomers, not obviously gifted as children. Bob Dylan did not stand out from other singers when he began his career.

Self-doubt comes with the territory. We hardly get started on our adventure before we feel faint of heart. Is this really what I want? Can I really pull it off? If I look back on nearly every worthwhile thing I have done—leaving home to attend Stanford as an undergraduate, moving to Seattle alone and without a job as a young adult, beginning the first edition of this book for Ten Speed Press—I remember moments of acute insecurity as I took stock and wondered, "Now why did I think that I wanted to do this again?" Often, it wasn't until later in my journey that my efforts seemed worthwhile.

> "What can be more satisfying than to be engaged in work in which every capacity or talent one may have is needed, every lesson one may have learned is used, every value one cares about is furthered?"
>
> **—JOHN GARDENER**

Most of us both do and do not want to set off on an adventure. We want to express our uniqueness, but we worry that our expressions may not be good enough in a competitive marketplace. My creative clients came to counseling because they had lost faith in themselves, mired down in depression or self-criticism or bad habits, but when I asked them why they wanted to get better, they said that they wanted to help other people, to share their experience, to give freely of their joy and love and talent. That goal gave them incentive to embark on an adventure of personal growth.

FULFILLING THE CALL

At this stage of the creative process you begin cultivating the gifts you have been given. You accept responsibility for obtaining whatever skills you need. You develop your talents through training: formal education, apprenticeship, independent study and reflection, daily practice, or whatever makes sense to you. You invest your time and energy and other resources to learn your craft and develop your skills. You labor with what you love.

Work that is well chosen for your abilities can feel much better than getting stoned or watching TV or doing nothing at all. Creative work is known for producing a state of flow, an altered state of consciousness in which you feel relaxed, unaware of the passage of time, and deeply absorbed in your efforts. Flow feels so good that people want to keep doing the activities that produce it. Curiously enough, of all the activities most likely to produce this flow state, the most common is work! Not any kind of work, obviously, but a kind of work that merges with play.

Creative work and play look surprisingly alike. They feel alike, too. Perhaps this is why creative people tend to say they are either always working or never working. Research has shown that people are happiest when they are fully engaged at a task that is intrinsically motivating and set at the frontier of their abilities.[55] In other words, when you find something you love to do and keep it challenging, work becomes joyous. A good example is the musician whose enjoyment in music continues to grow and deepen after years of disciplined effort.

Involvement in your chosen domain can become an upward spiral. Once baseline knowledge is established, it can be thrilling to learn more. The world expands as you continue to discover new things in your field. I experienced this on a small scale when we hired a landscape architect to help us beautify an eyesore in our backyard. Thanks to his work, I began to notice trees in a way I never had before, newly awakened to beauty that had always surrounded me.

Symbolic domains like music and art and literature remain pleasurable and challenging for as long as you live. You can always sing another song or paint a different landscape, learn new skills or add to your knowledge, and push the boundaries of your chosen art form. You'll never deplete your chosen domain. Plumb the depths, and they can provide you with pleasure that rivals big-ticket expenditures like a new sports car or two weeks at the beach. You don't need to be rich or famous or beautiful or powerful to feel good. You don't need to use drugs or have an affair.

> "The artist is nothing without the gift, but the gift is nothing without work."
>
> —ÉMILE ZOLA

You do need to keep your perspective, however. If the danger at the beginning of your journey lies in failing to accept your gifts, the danger in the middle is in making them the sole focus of your life. Creative people are vulnerable to overidentifying with

> "It is not the cunning careerist who wins in the end. It is the careful nurturer who tills his garden daily and grows the most natural, organic, and unforced flowers . . ."
>
> —HENRY GELDZAHLER

their talent and overinvesting in their work. The sensitivity that makes them special also makes it easier for them to become wounded, to go into a shell. One psychoanalyst wrote: "The tendency to wrap himself in a cloak of narcissistic self-love—because his art in its content is in greater or lesser degree a transformation of himself—in the event of outer rejection is a very powerful one. This is one of the sources of that excessive self-love which destroys art and artists."[56]

A very dear friend of mine made this mistake. A person of unusual intellectual and creative ability, he made being a writer his only identity and achieving recognition for his writing his only life goal. Perhaps

> "Society is downright savage to creative thinkers, especially when they are young."
>
> —ELLIS PAUL TORRANCE

because so much was at stake, he was hypersensitive to the inevitable criticism and rejection his work received. Gradually he withdrew from people and then he even stopped writing. Shortly after turning forty, he committed suicide. Certainly many factors influenced his suicide, but I believe one of them was shame that he had not received the recognition of his talent that he'd expected by midlife.

His tragic story contains lessons for us all. One lesson is the danger of depending on others for recognition. Recognition is sweet, and even sweeter if it comes from someone we admire. Unfortunately, someone important may not recognize your gift simply because she or he has different taste. Since your talent is most likely to be recognized by people who possess similar talent, you will fare better when you are surrounded by true peers, and we are not all lucky enough to be surrounded by true peers. People who lack knowledge of your field and appreciation for your art form may not realize that you have done any work of value at all.

> "The fact is that most people, groups, and organizations do not want you to be an original, independent, creative individual. They prefer that you be passive, easily manipulated, anxious to conform to existing practices, and not too successful."
>
> —JOHN CHAFFEE

Like my friend, we are vulnerable to becoming depressed if we put all our eggs in one basket. So another lesson is to spread your eggs out among several different baskets. Maintain old relationships but also make new friends; engage in exciting, creative, this-could-make-you-great projects as well as more ordinary, secure, but still satisfying projects. In other words, keep your connections balanced and varied. There are so many way to connect! Consider connecting to an online community, a Meetup group, a church or other faith-based community, your current workplace, an alma mater, a favorite sport, or a special cause.

> "You ain't going nowhere, son. You ought to go back to driving a truck."
>
> —THE GRAND OLE OPRY'S JIM DENNY TO ELVIS PRESLEY

You want to use your creative talents, but not to the exclusion of the rest of yourself. Richard Bolles, the author of *What Color Is Your Parachute?*, has a nice metaphor for this idea. Suppose that you are a chef, and you have been asked to use a tomato (your creative gift) in tonight's meal. You could use the tomato stuffed as a main course, stewed as a vegetable, tossed in a salad, or simply as a garnish to dress the plate. The important thing is to use it—along with other foods. You'd never want it to be the only food you served.

The middle of any adventure can be pretty tough going at times, because that's where you spend the most time and encounter the greatest adversity. You, too, will undoubtedly face difficulties on your path: grants that fall through; contracts canceled; poor ticket sales; not being able to find a job in your field; not having enough time to devote to creative tasks, even when you do have a creative job; and so on. The preceding chapter is designed to help you cope with adversity and persist in spite of such difficulties.

If the critics pan your performance or the publishers reject your manuscript, it's okay to retreat to a safe place and lick your wounds. Nurture and protect your creative spirit. Then, when you are ready, learn what you can from the experience and get back on the road. Learning from experience is one of my favorite definitions of intelligence, and I don't know a more positive way to cope.

RETURNING WITH A GIFT

Heroes return from adventure with something of benefit for others: a boon, a revelation, a vision, a gift. If you write a poem and have it published, that's sharing a gift. If you are a teacher who instills in your students a love of learning, that's sharing a gift. I still feel gratitude when I remember the gift given to me by the children's librarian in Longview, Washington, who took a respectful interest in my weekly visits fifty years ago and gently encouraged me to read something other than Nancy Drew.

Giving your gift becomes easier when you realize that other people struggle with the same problems you do. Especially when you are young, you feel alone. There was a time, for example, when I felt like I was the only one who didn't fit in. But when you look around, you will see that your personal problem is also a universal problem shared by other people, and you need to generalize your problem so that its solution has relevance for them. Expand your self-focus.

Those who work to benefit humanity typically feel happier than those who are more self-centered. Giving something back to the community usually feels good. People like your poem or your class or your book selection and tell you so. Some creators are exalted, receiving wealth and fame in return for their gifts. We live in the most pluralistic civilization ever, and even if your work is not universally admired, you can find an audience that will truly appreciate it.

> "I use my talent for writing, but I save my genius for living."
>
> —OSCAR WILDE

However, giving a gift also carries with it the threat of public censure and disapproval. Our culture seems to revere creativity and places it on a pedestal with other socially desirable attributes, such as intelligence, good looks, and extraversion. But society's response to creativity is, in fact, much more ambivalent. Think about what happened to exceptionally creative people such as Socrates, Jesus Christ, and Galileo. Most of us won't have to worry about being put to death or placed under house arrest, but we may still occasionally find ourselves very unpopular.

The danger in the final part of our journey lies in withholding our gifts because we fear we'll be unpopular or disliked or criticized. Just as Socrates was a gadfly to society, creators are both irritants and catalysts to the conventional world. We creators need to remember that it's human nature to be upset when the status quo is challenged—and this is true even when that challenge results in changes that are later glorified as wonderful progress.

I encourage you to offer your gifts even if you may face some unfair criticism in return. It's all part of the process. Criticism often arises not because people are intentionally cruel but because they are human beings who don't like change. I don't always adore new ideas myself. When someone conventional has a very negative reaction to one of my ideas and I feel hurt, I tell myself that I must be on target or I wouldn't be getting such an emotional response. In fact, it has often been my experience that someone who is initially very negative later comes around to appreciate the idea very much.

You can trust and take part in this process. Your gifts will be awakened when you are in the presence of a master. The problems will find you. Your problems will be other people's problems, as well. Your task is to accept your gifts and your problems. Discipline your talent. Generalize your experience. Take risks. Risk investing in the development of your talent, even though you lack any assurance of return. Risk giving something of yourself, even though others may not respond positively.

IT'S A CYCLICAL PROCESS

Experts are now predicting about twelve changes during the average person's working life. Their predictions are probably for people doing conventional work. I'm persuaded (although I haven't seen any data to support this) that creative people are likely to change and cycle through jobs even more often than that. By nature they are more restless, more easily bored, and more motivated by learning and personal growth. They need more variety.

At this point you may be wondering what "career adventure" means for you. You're not sure how much priority you should give to your creative endeavors and how much you should give to a secure job with a decent income. You don't know whether following your bliss means starting a new hobby that fits into your schedule or making a radical change, like going back to school to study journalism.

> "The sour truth is that I am imprisoned with a perception which will settle for nothing less than making a revolution in the consciousness of our time."
>
> **—NORMAN MAILER**

The questions may be more important than the answers, for the answers keep evolving and aren't so much right or wrong as different ways to proceed with different advantages and disadvantages. Let the questions beckon you to adventure. Cast aside the "shoulds" regarding your career—such as "You should know what you want to do with your life," or "You should stick with your first choice forever"—and make the best choices you can right now. As vocational psychologist John Krumboltz advises: test your dreams one step at a time.

I have it on good authority that you can trust the process. When I came to the end of long-term counseling with a client, or to the end of a year of supervising a psychology intern, I usually asked that person what he or she had learned. I have heard one answer more than all the others combined: "I learned to trust the process." Once people have come through a change and begin to feel safe and more secure on the other side, they realize that the process of growth deserved more of their confidence from the outset.

> "Be patient with all that is unsolved in your heart. And try to love the questions themselves. . . . Don't search for the answers, which could not be given to you now because you would not be able to live them. And the point is, to live everything. . . . Live the questions now."
>
> **—RAINER MARIA RILKE**

Because you will always be changing and growing as a person, you'll probably find that satisfying your creative urge is not simply a matter of finding an ideal job and living happily ever after. Instead, finding new outlets for your creativity is likely to be an ongoing challenge. One artist I know moved from business to graphic design to painting, all within the space of a few years. It is typical of creative people, even those who are very successful, to want more than is provided in their jobs. Think of the TV stars who abandon roles that look to outsiders like the pinnacle of success.

A career adventure focuses on problems to which the answers are never final. As you embody conflicts and grow through them, you realize more of your potential; then, from a more mature perspective, you are again faced with the inevitable tensions that are part of being human. Creators often find themselves circling back, revisiting themes they have already explored, but with a broader perspective. (Small wonder that psychological growth is so often described as helical in shape!) There are always new gifts and new problems that emerge and need to be integrated, no matter how much development has already taken place.

Clearly, it's not easy to sustain a creative career adventure. It's a heroic undertaking. There will be times when your adventure is wonderfully fun and exciting, and other times when you need to call on your courage. In one of my favorite passages about creativity, psychologist Donald MacKinnon emphasizes the importance of courage for the creator:

> *"The most salient mark of a creative person, the central trait at the core of his being is, as I see it, just this sort of courage. It is not physical courage of the type that might be rewarded by the Carnegie Medal or the Congressional Medal of Honor, although a creative person may have courage of this kind, too. Rather, it is personal courage, courage of the mind and spirit, psychological or spiritual courage that is the radix of a creative person: the courage to question what is generally accepted; the courage to be destructive in order that something better can be constructed; the courage to think thoughts unlike anyone else's; the courage to be open to experience both from within and from without; the courage to imagine the impossible and try to achieve it; the courage to stand aside from the collectivity and in conflict with it if necessary, the courage to become and to be oneself."*[57]

IT TAKES COURAGE TO BE YOURSELF

Otto Rank was an early psychologist who wrote about the psychological development of the creative person. According to Rank, there are three kinds of people. He said the *average* person conforms to society to the exclusion of expressing his or her individuality, and the *neurotic* person expresses his or her individuality to the exclusion of being part of society. Only the *artistic* person successfully integrates the two conflicting roles. A later writer summarized Rank's ideas as follows: "The ideal of the average is to be as others are; of the 'neurotic,' to be himself largely in opposition to what others want him to be; of the creative person, to be that which he actually is."[58]

> "You need to keep your eye on the ball, not Babe Ruth."
>
> —NANCY PACKER

> "I did not make my songs, my songs made me."
>
> —JOHANN WOLFGANG VON GOETHE

I suppose it would be easier for all of us to be the people we truly are if we didn't inherit so many prejudices about the kind of person we think we should be. These internal "shoulds" may be the fiercest lions and tigers and bears you ever encounter. One of my favorite American novels is *Invisible Man* by Ralph Ellison. The invisible man is an African American and a Southerner who, after trying very hard and unsuccessfully to become the kind of person he thought he should be, concludes, "I yam what I yam." A different story is told about Rabbi Zusha of Hannipol, who lived his life complaining about his lack of talent and reproaching himself for not being just like Moses. God said to him, "In the coming world, we will not ask you why you were not Moses, but why you were not Zusha."

One of the things I learned as a result of writing this book is to honor creativity in many different forms, both within myself and as a part of everybody I know. A literary snob, I used to think that if I couldn't be Jane Austen, I might as well not write. Despite positive feedback from others, I did not take my writing seriously or appreciate how my empathic abilities could help me as a writer. Now that I have gone through the process of writing this book, I'm more appreciative that I can make a contribution even if I'm not Jane Austen—and I'm able to look at other people and their gifts with less prejudice as well.

Perhaps the person you are doesn't fit your image of the person you want to be. If so, try to recognize and honor your uniqueness. Nancy McCarthy, a career counselor in the fashion industry, told me that she originally wanted to be an architect, but she didn't have the three-dimensional spatial ability an architect needs. Now she sees herself as having other remarkable gifts and making a greater contribution than she would have made as an architect. John Holland was an Artistic type who gave up aspirations to be a concert pianist because he lacked sufficient musical memory. Instead, he played the piano at home and devoted his genius to the development of a career theory that has helped millions of people and will doubtless help millions more.

You, too, may originally have been inspired by a career choice that was too limiting, perhaps because there were some pieces missing in your understanding of yourself. As you continue your journey, your character will strengthen and your self-knowledge will grow, and you can let go of earlier and simpler ideas that prove to be too confining. What you now think you are going after may not turn out to be the greatest thing you achieve.

It's the challenge of a lifetime: love your fate. Pursue your unconventional goals. Have an adventure. You are the artist of your own life. Here's how religious writer Marcus Bach describes the philosophy that life is art:

> "I am the artist! I am the master craftsman shaping my existence from the cradle to the grave. I wield the tools, dream the dreams, see the visions, draw the plans, take the time, do the work in everything I say and think every moment of the day. As a sculptor takes his raw material and begins to realize the ideal, or idealize the real, as a painter takes his brush and gives form to his creative idea, so in total life I am the artist!"[59]

OUR WORLD NEEDS YOUR WORK

Creative work brings things together at many levels. Creative thinking brings information together in a new product. Creative activities bring together different parts of yourself, reclaiming parts that have grown unfamiliar through disuse. A creative approach to life-work planning can bring different kinds of work together in a new career, particularly at those connecting points where you join your personal interests and talents and values in ways no one ever has before.

> "Vision is the art of seeing things invisible."
>
> —JONATHAN SWIFT

> "All art has this characteristic—it unites people."
>
> —LEO TOLSTOY

As we begin the twenty-first century on an overpopulated planet, our problems are staggering. Every day we are confronted with crises, conflict, and chaos. War. Global warming. Terrorism. Drug abuse. Poverty. Epidemics. World hunger. In addition to the huge problems, there are smaller-scale problems in our own homes or communities. We surely need the power of creativity to solve problems for which we have no ready-made solutions. We also need help finding a unity that honors our burgeoning diversity.

I'd like to close with a focus not on your needs and growth as an individual, but on the needs of our world for your creative talent. As creators, we do more than create our own lives—we create the world we live in. We are shaped by our culture and, in turn, we shape it. The danger here is that we won't take action because we are waiting for someone else to take care of our community problems for us.

The human tendency to wait for others to take care of us is exemplified in a tragic story. In 1977 at Tenerife Airport in the Canary Islands, an incoming plane struck a plane full of passengers on the runway. In the chaos and confusion that ensued, many people remained in their seats, presumably waiting for flight attendants or other authorities to come and tell them what to do. A few passengers took matters into their own hands, clambering over tops of seats and jumping off the wing. Some broke bones in the fall, but they lived. Those who waited in their seats perished in flames that soon engulfed the plane.

In some ways our world is like that plane on the runway at Tenerife. We are faced with grave problems that require creative solutions, and we wait for someone else to help us, at our peril. Participate! Don't let yourself project your responsibility onto someone else, such as a professional artist or an already established hero. Creative activities are not just for celebrities.

> "We have to take life—society and human relations—more or less as we find them. The only thing that we can really make is our work. And deliberate work of the mind, imagination and hand, done, as Nietzsche said, 'notwithstanding,' in the long run remakes the world."
>
> —EDMUND WILSON

Not only in our personal lives, but also for our culture, we can offer a spiritual perspective. Artistic work is spiritual, a personal meditation that provides food for the soul of others. Creative work connects us to what is fundamental and enduring and eternal. One of the things I appreciate most about art is its transcendent quality, its ability to raise consciousness to a higher level. After I encounter a work of art, my vision is cleared. The small troubles over which I had felt peevish and upset no longer seem so important. My consciousness has been raised, and I am grateful.

There is something spiritual in the act of bringing things together, making them whole. And we always need to bring things together, because humans tend to divide, to label, to distort. We can't help but perceive through filters and biases. I was reminded of this time and time again when I was nursing my infant son. I would look into his eyes and see my face reflected there and immediately think, "I look awful." And then I would realize that of course

I didn't look awful to him. He had no conception of beauty. He had not yet learned to think, "Mama's got nice eyes, but her hair is flat." And then I would realize that I looked just like what I was—a person with many nights of broken sleep and no time to wash her hair.

Astronauts have a similar shift in perspective when they look at our planet from space. Michael Collins of Apollo 11 said, "The Earth is one unit. You don't have the feeling that it's a fragmented place, that it's divided up into countries. You can't see any people, you can't hear any noise. It just seems like a very small, fragile, serene little sphere. It makes you wish that it really were as serene as it appears. It makes you wonder what any of us might do to make it a happier and more peaceful place."[60]

> "The most important function of art and science is to awaken the cosmic religious feeling and keep it alive."
>
> —ALBERT EINSTEIN

> "A poet's function—do not be startled by this remark—is not to experience the poetic state: that is a private affair. His function is to create it in others."
>
> —PAUL VALÉRY

As Joseph Campbell said, our culture needs new myths, a new vision of what could be. As creative people, we can provide a new vision. We can find ways to creatively express for others the abstract ideas that we value. In so doing, we gain a sense of purpose and meaning that transcends the maintenance of the physical and economic self. We serve a higher cause.

I've come to believe that conventional thinkers are limited in their ability to tolerate anxiety. Many people don't have the courage to admit a potentially troublesome reality, and they protect themselves from emotional upset by denying that trouble really exists. It is the gift of creative people to have the strength of character to subject ourselves to such anxiety for the good of others. They may think we are crazy, when we are simply allowing ourselves to see and feel and communicate more complexity—both more of the positives and more of the negatives—than they have the courage to confront.

It is our job to help them see. As artists we can shift the perspective of our world. We can help others see or hear or feel afresh. Locally and globally we can reunite what has been forced apart by old ways of thinking that have become destructive. Ours is not an easy role, because it requires taking risks, meeting opposition, and perhaps not earning financial rewards equal to our contribution. But our role is vital. We can all make meaningful and valuable contributions, in our own ways.

We have come to the end of our journey together. Ahead of us lies nameless, faceless, formless reality—a jumble of complexity waiting for you to give it form and meaning. I'll say good-bye to you here. I expect that you will continue on your adventure, struggling with worthy problems and emerging a stronger person than when you began. I hope you will give form to your personal vision and share it with us all.

LEGEND OF SYMBOLS

➡ These occupations require the most complex use of information, which allows the greatest creativity.

■ These occupations may also require a high level of skill with things, even though they're not on the Ideas and Things path.

The Career Reference Section:
281 OCCUPATIONS FOR CREATIVE AND UNCONVENTIONAL PEOPLE

Unless otherwise noted, if annual wages are not given, these figures are either difficult to obtain or highly variable, ranging from under $20,000 to over $100,000. Median wages in 2013 were primarily obtained from the U.S. Department of Labor, O*NET OnLine (www.onetonline.org), or the Bureau of Labor Statistics (www.bls.gov). These are reliable sources; nevertheless, I'd recommend that you verify income information. For example, the O*Net website declares an income of more than $50,000 for creative writers, including poets—yet I do not personally know of any poets that make nearly that much money from their poetry! When you find an occupation of interest, take time to do some research to learn more about the median salaries.

All of the following occupations have a three-letter Holland code. Please remember that you are not looking for a perfectly aligned three-letter correspondence to your own code but for an overlap of some of the letters with your own code. In fact, the codes that follow should be considered an approximation, because Holland codes are not consistent among various sources. Additionally, job titles and associated job requirements are not constant across organizations. Therefore, it is important to carefully review the information for the particular occupation you are considering and then get more information, to confirm a match with your requirements.

Path 1
IDEAS

WRITERS

Arranger (AEI) ➡

Arrangers transcribe musical compositions, adapting, reworking, and arranging them to accommodate different musical styles. They select voice, rhythm, tempo, instrument, and other features of a song. Arrangers are hired by the recording industry, music directors, music publishers, music services, print-music licensees, theater groups, and performing artists. Arrangers usually freelance and are sometimes paid royalties. The median annual wage in 2013 was $48,330.

Biographer (ASE) ➡

Biographers specialize in writing reconstructions of the lives of individuals, including both psychological and historical influences on a subject's story. They base their narratives on a variety of biographical sources, such as diaries, letters, news articles, and interviews with relatives. Biographers are hired by celebrities, families, and publishers of books and magazines.

Blogger (AEI) ➡

Bloggers write web logs, known as blogs, and publish them online. They research a topic, develop their own unique style and/or subject matter, write and edit their own content, and produce blog posts, which are published at regular intervals, such as once a day or twice a month. They may use media tools, so they can edit and produce their content via audio and video. Bloggers are typically self-employed; those with large followings may have waited many years to derive income from advertising, sponsorships, speaking fees, or sales of products such as books. Some bloggers contract their services to various companies; some are employed by print media.

Columnist/Commentator (AES) ➡

Columnists write columns for magazines, newspapers, and websites; commentators write commentary that is taped or presented live on TV or radio. These writers gather, analyze, and interpret information to develop a personal perspective on their subject matter. They may specialize in a particular field, such as politics, health, sports, or gardening. Columnists and commentators are employed by newspapers, magazines, websites, and radio and TV stations.

Composer (ASE) ➡

Composers write original musical compositions such as operas, symphonies, and popular songs. They also transcribe their ideas into musical notation, sometimes using a computer to help them compose and edit their work. Composers work for record companies, recording groups, performing artists, production companies, and producers of opera and theatrical musical plays. They may also write music for radio, TV, and film. The median annual wage in 2013 was $48,330.

Continuity Writer (AES) ➡

Continuity writers write original scripts for TV or radio stations. Their scripts are read by an announcer to introduce, connect, and conclude the different parts of TV or radio programs as diverse as sports programs, nature shows, and musical events.

Copywriter (ASI) ➡

Copywriters develop original ideas for advertising campaigns, writing the text of advertisements that appear in print media and scripts for broadcast media, as well as mail-order and other catalogs. They research the product or service they are advertising, consult with their clients, and perhaps review marketing trends for comparable products or services. Copywriters are employed by advertising agencies, direct marketing agencies, and in-house advertising departments at large companies and corporations. An increasing number are self-employed. The median annual wage in 2013 was $57,750.

Critic (AES) ➡

Critics write reviews of artistic, literary, musical, and other events for print, online, and broadcast media. They analyze the work, compare it to other works, and evaluate it against objective standards, basing their opinions on knowledge, personal experience, and judgment. Specialties include art, books, dance, drama, food, movies, online media, and music. Critics are employed at newspapers, magazines, and radio and TV stations.

Crossword-Puzzle Maker (ASE) ➡

Crossword-puzzle makers create crossword puzzles, including numbered lists of short definitions and completed puzzles that show the correct solution. After drawing and designing numbered blank squares, they choose words to fit the open spaces so that the spelling coincides both horizontally and vertically. Crossword-puzzle makers are hired by publishers of newspapers, magazines, and books.

Editorial Writer (AES) ➡

Editorial writers examine the issues and topics that are generated by news events. Combining their views with the official position of their publications, they write editorials to influence public opinion. They may help determine the editorial positions of their publication or decide on the contents of the editorial pages. Some specialize in a particular area such as politics, international affairs, or financial matters. Editorial writers are employed by newspapers and news services. The median annual wage in 2013 was $57,750.

Humorist (ASE) ➡

Humorists write amusing material for performers. After receiving or selecting a topic, they write and revise the material until it meets their clients' approval. Some specialize in writing comedy shows or comedy routines for entertainers. Humorists may work for radio and TV shows. Many are self-employed.

Librettist (ASE) ➡

Librettists write the text of full-length dramatic stories that are set to music composed by someone else. They develop the story, adapting their text to fit the needs of composers and singers. They are employed by producers of operas and musicals.

Lyricist (ASE) ➡

Lyricists write lyrics to accompany a melody written by someone else. They may be employed by performing artists, producers, record companies, recording groups, or advertising agencies. The median annual wage in 2013 for poets, lyricists, and creative writers was $57,750.

Orchestrator (AEI) ➡

Orchestrators transpose an existing musical score so that it better accommodates the abilities of particular instrumental and vocal musicians. Orchestrators are hired by producers of plays, movies, and

TV shows. They also work for orchestras, bands, choral groups, arrangers, and individual musicians. The median annual wage in 2013 for music arrangers was $48,330.

Playwright (ASE) ➡

Playwrights write scripts for plays that are usually intended to be performed on stage. They write dialogue and describe action to be taken, then revise the script during the time it is being rehearsed and prepared for production. Playwrights are employed by theater groups and producers of TV and motion pictures. They also sell their work to publishers. The median annual wage in 2013 for poets, lyricists, and creative writers was $57,750.

Poet (AES) ➡

Poets write poetry and sell their work to publishers of books, greeting cards, and magazines, including literary and academic journals. The median annual wage in 2013 for poets, lyricists, and creative writers was $57,750.

Reader (AES)

A reader (also known as a story analyst) reads plays, stories, novels, and screenplays and writes a synopsis to be reviewed by the producer or editorial staff. They evaluate whether the story would adapt well to a visual medium. Once dramatic material is chosen for development, readers may recommend possible treatments. They work for literary agencies, film and TV studios, associate producers, independent movie production companies, and even individual stars. Freelance script readers earn $40 to $60 per script; freelance book readers earn $25 to $100 per manuscript. Readers who join the Studio Readers Union work for major studios and are paid $27.89 to $33.52 per hour.

Reporter (ASI)

Reporters gather and analyze information about news events and write stories for print, online, or broadcast media. They research the news, verify the accuracy of their information, organize and focus the material, and write a story following editorial standards. Radio reporters may read their story on the air. TV reporters may also direct a film crew, appear on TV, and give live reports at the site of breaking news. Reporters are employed by online magazines and newspapers and radio and TV stations. The median annual wage in 2013 was $35,600.

Researcher (IAS)

Researchers often have a background in library science and are also known as information specialists or information brokers. They retrieve, analyze, and prepare information from a variety of sources (such as online databases, periodical articles, marketing surveys, government statistics) for written reports and oral presentations geared toward a professional audience. They may present information using statistical tables, graphs, and abstracts. They may freelance or be employed by libraries, universities, think tanks, legal and political firms, medical and scientific organizations, government agencies, and corporations.

Screenwriter (AEI) ➡

Screenwriters write scripts and screenplays for video, radio, and film. They may prepare an outline and summary before writing the entire script and then consult with the producer and director as they develop and revise the script. Screenwriters may collaborate with other writers and may adapt material from other genres. Screenwriters are hired by TV networks, radio stations, film studios, production companies, or corporate media centers; many freelance. The median annual wage in 2013 for poets, lyricists, and creative writers was $57,750.

Writer—Fiction and Nonfiction (AIE) ➡

Writers write original prose. They research a topic, organize their material, and develop and focus their ideas as they write and revise. Writers of nonfiction may specialize in a certain field; writers of fiction, in a certain genre. **Technical writers** translate scientific and technical information into understandable reports, user's manuals, and assorted publications. Writers are employed by industry, business, magazine publishers, media companies, educational institutions, consulting firms, and government agencies. They often freelance to special and general interest magazines, book publishers, and advertising and public-relations agencies. In 2013, the median annual wage for creative writers was $57,750; for technical writers, it was $67,900.

DIRECTORS

Artist and Repertoire Manager (AES)

A&R managers choose performing artists and musical compositions to be recorded. Based on their knowledge of public taste, popular music, and performing techniques, they audition and select the most appropriate performers and pieces. Some managers direct recording sessions and promote CD sales. A&R managers work for recording studios, record companies, and radio stations. Some are self-employed.

Book Editor (AES) ➡

Book editors acquire manuscripts, edit them, and guide them through the production process. They read submissions, recommend acquisition based on what they anticipate to be market demand, and negotiate terms of agreement. Editors may supervise an editorial staff and develop ideas for books. They contribute ideas to authors and coordinate activities of the design, production, and publicity departments. Book editors are employed by publishing houses. They often work freelance on various aspects of the editorial process, such as acquisitions or copyediting. The median annual wage in 2013 was $54,150.

Bureau Chief (AES) ➡

Bureau chiefs work for newspapers or press syndicates in foreign countries or distant locations. They direct the work of people who gather and edit news stories and photos to be transmitted back to the home office. Bureau chiefs may need to translate news dispatches into English. They may also do some reporting.

Choral Director (AES) ➡

Choral directors conduct groups of singers, such as church choirs and glee clubs. After auditioning members and choosing music that fits both the occasion and the ability of the group, they direct them during rehearsals and performances. Some choral directors are involved in planning tours, scheduling performances, and arranging for group travel. Choral directors are hired by churches, universities, other religious and educational institutions, symphonies, choirs, and other musical groups. The median annual wage in 2013 was $48,330.

Creative Director (AES) ➡

Creative directors develop the basic presentation for an advertisement, coordinating the work of the creative staff who write the copy and lay out the design. After reviewing information and discussing different options, they meet with heads of art, copywriting, and production departments to outline the basic concept, set a schedule, and attend to other client needs. Later they approve the promotional material that has been developed by the staff and present the final package to the client. Creative directors work for advertising agencies, direct marketing agencies, corporate advertising departments, and large media companies serving newspapers, magazines, and radio and TV stations. The median annual wage in 2013 was $83,000.

Cue Selector (ASE) ➡

Cue selectors work for television producers, integrating prerecorded music with the story line to arrange the musical score for an episode of a television series. Cue selectors read the script and confer with the director to establish the mood or effect desired. After listening to the music, they select appropriate passages and develop a tentative score. They then watch the episode and direct technical personnel to electronically record the score so that it supports the action.

Dictionary Editor (AIS) ➡

Dictionary editors, also known as lexicographers, compile and edit dictionaries. In addition to defining the meaning of new words, they write and review definitions. They conduct their own research, or direct the research of others, to discover the origin, spelling, syllabication, pronunciation, meaning, and usage of words. Some dictionary editors may also select drawings or other graphical elements to illustrate word meaning. Most are employed by publishers of dictionaries; some work for the federal government and large computer companies. The median annual wage in 2013 was $54,150.

Greeting Card Editor (AES) ➡

Greeting card editors choose and develop material for greeting card publishers. They read, evaluate, and edit original submissions from writers. They may coordinate the activities of those who design and print cards; they may sometimes write and design cards as well.

Magazine or Journal Editor (AES) ➡

Magazine editors are employed by magazines and journals to read, acquire, write, and edit stories and articles. They may supervise writers and coordinate the work of different departments. Some editors are subject matter specialists (for example, the fashion editor); others are responsible for the overall editorial content of a publication. The median annual wage for editors in 2013 was $54,150.

Motion Picture Director (ASE) ➡

Motion picture directors read and interpret a script, conduct rehearsals, and direct the activities of a cast and technical crew to film a motion picture. They schedule the sequence of scenes to be filmed, rehearse the cast, and direct the cast and technicians, as well as the art director and director of photography. Motion picture directors may be self-employed or may be hired by motion picture producers, film studios, and independent film production companies. The median annual wage in 2013 was $69,480.

Music Director (AES) ➡

Music directors conduct the orchestra during a recording or broadcast and direct the people who work in a studio music department. They choose music to suit the movie or show, perhaps hiring a composer to write a score. After auditioning and hiring musicians and other orchestra personnel, they assign such tasks as scoring, arranging, and writing lyrics. Music directors are hired by TV and motion picture producers. The median annual wage in 2013 was $48,330.

Music Producer (EAS) ➡

Music producers advise, guide, and coordinate the activities of musicians throughout the production process for recording music as well as producing live music events. Producers can be involved in song selection, musical arrangement of pieces, coordinating rehearsals, and even arranging financing. Music producers have strong musical backgrounds as well as a keen ability to create projects that will generate revenue for the artists involved. The median annual wage in 2013 was $69,480.

News Editor (AES) ➡

News editors work for newspapers, planning the layout of each edition. They decide where stories should be placed, balancing each story's significance with space constraints and design principles. They discuss placement of developing stories with other newspaper staff members. News editors may also edit copy and write or revise headlines. The median annual wage in 2013 was $54,150.

Orchestra Conductor (AES) ➡

Orchestra conductors conduct groups of instrumental musicians. After auditioning members and positioning them to achieve balance, they choose a repertoire that suits the occasion and the group and then direct them during rehearsal and performance. Some orchestra conductors organize tours, schedule performances, and arrange for group travel and accommodations. Orchestra conductors work for dance bands, symphony orchestras, opera or ballet companies, chamber ensembles, community orchestras, youth orchestras, conservatories, and schools with strong music departments. The median annual wage for music arrangers in 2013 was $48,330.

Religious Director (EAS)

Religious directors develop and direct church school programs for a denominational group. They analyze the educational needs of their congregation and collaborate with others in the ministry to establish programs and encourage participation. They may select curricula, publicize programs, schedule special events, allocate resources, recruit volunteers, and handle administrative details. Some directors also provide counseling for their congregation. Religious directors are hired by congregation organizations. The median annual wage in 2013 was $38,160.

Stage Director (AES) ➡

Stage directors direct an acting cast and technical crew, bringing to life their interpretation of a script or play. They rehearse the cast and guide actors and actresses to an opening performance consistent with their vision; they also coordinate other creative parts of the production, such as music, choreography, lighting, scenery, and costume design. Some directors also audition and hire the cast. An **artistic director** might play a similar role for a dance company. Stage directors work in regional theaters, dinner theaters, repertory companies, and stock companies. The median annual wage in 2013 was $69,480.

PERFORMERS

Acrobat (AER) ➡

Acrobats entertain an audience by performing spectacular feats that may include balancing, juggling, and tumbling. Performing alone or with others, they may adapt stock routines or create original acts. Acrobats are employed by circuses and may occasionally find work with theater companies and theme parks or through event-planning services or entertainment agencies.

Actor (AES) ➡

Actors interpret the words and actions of a character in a script. After reading and rehearsing the script, they entertain an audience with their portrayal of their role, creating character through gestures, facial expressions, props, and perhaps even song and dance. Actors and actresses may work on the stage and in professional regional theaters, dinner theaters, stock companies, and repertory companies. Network entertainment centers and local TV stations provide employment opportunities in TV. Motion pictures, industrial films, radio, nightclubs, theme parks, advertising agencies, and party-planning services also employ actors and actresses. Some actors even work in courtrooms, reenacting the testimony of witnesses who won't appear in court. The median hourly wage reported in O*NET OnLine for an actor in 2013 was $22.15, although wages can vary greatly depending on whether the actor is performing in a local production, in film or television, or in a Broadway play.

Announcer (AES)

Announcers speak on television or radio. After gathering and preparing information so that it will fit the time allowed, they deliver news, sports, and weather. They may also talk about breaking news, announce station breaks or commercials, describe public events or sporting events, plan and prepare for upcoming programs, host charitable events, and make promotional appearances for the radio and TV stations that employ them. Median wages for announcers in 2013 were $13.95 hourly and $29,020 annually.

Clown (EAC) ➡

Dressed in costumes and makeup, clowns entertain audiences by performing original routines or stock slapstick, using such skills as juggling, pantomime, walking on stilts, riding a unicycle, and creating balloon sculptures. Most clowns are employed by circus producers, amusement parks, and TV or film producers, but self-employed clowns find work through entertainment agencies and event-planning services, as well as trade shows and conventions. They also freelance at birthday parties, banquets, and rodeos.

Comedian (AES) ➡

Comedians amuse their audiences by telling jokes and performing monologues. They may also sing, dance, and make funny faces. Comedians find work through talent agencies, entertainment agencies, party-planning agencies, TV producers, and owners or managers of comedy clubs, nightclubs, hotels, lounges, theme parks, and cruise ships.

Dancer (AER) ➡

Dancers may specialize in one style of dancing, such as ballet, tap, ballroom, folk, jazz, or modern. They are employed by dance companies and producers of TV shows and commercials, music videos, movies, musical comedy, and opera. Dancers also work in nightclubs, hotels, resorts, cruise ships, theme parks, and industrial exhibitions. The median hourly wage in 2013 was $14.87.

Disc Jockey (AES)

Disc jockeys, also known as on-air personalities, announce musical selections on a radio program. They select the music to be played, read commercials, introduce station breaks, and also comment in an entertaining way on matters of interest to their listeners. They may specialize in one type of music, such as country or classical. They may interview musicians or individuals from their listening audience. The median hourly wage in 2013 was $13.95 or $29,020 annually, but annual wages for popular on-air personalities in large markets can be more than $100,000. Many disc jockeys, generally known as DJs, are self-employed and hired by dance clubs, private parties, and event planners to select and play dance music. Self-employment wages vary widely depending on location, quality of equipment, and the niche in which services are provided.

Double (AER)

Doubles portray stars of motion pictures or TV movies. Dressing in the same costume as the star, they imitate the performer's gestures and mannerisms, either facing away from the camera or at a distance from the camera. Doubles are employed by film and television producers and studios.

Equestrian (AER)

Equestrians entertain an audience by riding horses while performing acrobatic stunts or other feats of skill and daring. **Bareback riders** perform on horses without saddles. Equestrians work at circuses, carnivals, horse shows, and other exhibitions.

Impersonator (AES) ➡

Impersonators imitate people, animals, or inanimate objects. They entertain an audience by mimicking the voice, sound, physical form, expression, or mannerisms of their subject. Impersonators find work through nightclubs, talent agencies, entertainment agencies, party-planning services, theme parks, and TV producers.

Mime (AEI) ➡

Mimes entertain an audience through pantomime. Using only body movements, gestures, and facial expressions, they portray tragic and comic moods and dramatic situations. Mimes freelance, finding work through entertainment agencies and event-planning services.

Narrator (AES) ➡

Narrators provide their voice talents to dramatic and educational productions on film, video or audiotape, and compact disc. For example, they might read from a script to narrate travelogues, documentaries, books on tape, or animated cartoons. Narrators are employed by television and motion picture studios, recording studios, and production companies.

Ring Conductor (EAS)

Ring conductors work for circuses, introducing acts in a style requested by the management. Using a schedule of performances, they announce the beginning and ending of individual acts and signal the performers to create smooth transitions between acts. In the event of an accident or other emergency, they handle the concerns of the audience.

Show Host (EAS)

Show hosts guide a talk show or game show on radio or TV. They first confer with the producer to select a topic, then read background information to prepare a program. During the show, they may interview guests, discuss topics over the phone with listeners, manage the play of the game, and describe or demonstrate products. Talk and game show hosts are employed by radio and television stations.

Singer (AES) ➡

Singers are often classified according to the range of their voices, such as soprano or tenor, and they may specialize in singing particular types of music, such as opera, folk, rock, religious, or country and western. Some singers provide studio backup for better-known recording artists. **Karaoke singers** perform with a karaoke system (their focus may be less on singing and more on helping the audience enjoy the party). Singers are hired by managers of nightclubs and lounges and by producers of musical entertainment, such as operas, musicals, dinner theaters, regional theaters, variety shows, cruise ships, and recording studios. The median hourly wage in 2013 was $23.74.

Storyteller (ASE) ➡

Storytellers tell stories, usually to a live audience. After background reading, they develop a personal story or choose a suitable story or folk tale. Using eye contact and sometimes clothing and props, they invite audience participation in a way that helps the listeners create their own images of the action. Storytellers are hired by schools, libraries, folklore centers, entertainment agencies, and other planners of parties, conferences, and festivals.

Ventriloquist (AES) ➡

Ventriloquists manipulate a dummy or puppet so that it appears to be alive and project their voices so that it appears to talk. They may also create the dummy and write the script for their performance. They find work through entertainment agencies and event-planning services.

Wire Walker (AER)

Wire walkers, also known as high-wire artists or tightrope walkers, are employed by circuses. They perform on a high wire or rope or cable, walking or riding bikes or performing stunts—such as headstands or somersaults—that require balance and acrobatic skill.

INVESTIGATORS

Anthropologist (IAR) ➡ ■

Anthropologists study the origins, physical development, and cultural behavior of human beings. They design research studies, gather and analyze data, and then write about and present their findings and conclusions. Specialties include archeology and physical, social, or cultural anthropology in different regions of the world. Applied anthropologists may apply scientific concepts to current problems, such as giving advice on the cultural impact of public policy. The median annual wage in 2013 was $58,360.

Architectural Historian (IAR) ■

Architectural historians study the history of architecture, researching and recording important buildings in order to preserve them. They identify, photograph, and document historic structures, study the neighboring area, decide which properties are important enough to be designated as historic, and prepare detailed reports. Specialties include planning and administration, field research and evaluation, historic site curatorship, and management of Main Street programs. Architectural historians are employed by architectural and consulting firms; federal, state, and city governments; museums; educational institutions; archival centers; and nonprofit organizations. Some architectural historians are self-employed. In 2009, salaries ranged from $30,000 for those with minimal training and experience to $79,000 for those with advanced training and more than five years of experience.

Biologist (IAR) ➡ ■

Biologists study plants and animals and how they relate to their environment. Some biologists conduct research in the field, which could be anywhere from tropical rainforests to alpine tundra. Others work in research laboratories with sophisticated technical equipment. Biologists may specialize in areas such as botany, zoology, ecology, or marine biology. Biologists are employed by educational institutions, hospitals, research laboratories, the government, and the pharmaceutical industry. The median annual wages in 2013 were $57,430 for wildlife biologists and zoologists and $67,840 for microbiologists.

Economist (IAS) ➡

Economists study the production and distribution of goods and services, planning and conducting research to analyze costs and benefits. They collect and analyze data, then develop forecasts, prepare reports, formulate recommendations, and advise clients. Many economists apply economic principles to data in a particular area, such as agriculture, health, labor, the environment, or international trade. Economists work for banks, government agencies, economic research firms, management consulting firms, securities and commodities brokers, computer and data-processing companies, and colleges and universities. The median annual wage in 2013 was $93,070.

Experimental Psychologist (IAE) ➡ ■

Experimental psychologists study human and animal behavior through the experimental method, planning and conducting psychological studies and then analyzing the results. They formulate hypotheses and design experiments to investigate problems in areas such as motivation, memory, learning, or substance use. After conducting the experiments, they interpret the data and write a report. Experimental psychologists are employed by colleges and universities, government agencies, research organizations, ergonomics industries, and consulting firms. The median annual wage for post-secondary psychology faculty in 2013 was $68,980. The American Psychological Association reports annual wages for doctoral-level experimental psychologists ranging from $76,090 to $116,343.

Flavor Chemist (IAR) ➡ ■

Flavorists, also known as flavor chemists or flavor scientists, blend aroma chemicals, essential oils, botanical extracts, and essences to create natural and artificial flavorings for a variety of products (foods, beverages, medications, cosmetics, pet foods, and the like). After researching a naturally existing flavor, they attempt to duplicate it using mathematics, chemistry, and artistry to produce a longer-lasting, better-tasting flavor that can withstand commercial preparation. Flavor formulations are laboratory tested as well as taste tested. Food and beverage and pharmaceutical companies may employ some flavorists, but most are employed by flavor houses. According to the Bureau of Labor Statistics, the median annual wage for all chemists in 2012 was $78,870. Payscale.com reports 2014 earnings for food chemists, a group that includes flavor chemists, ranging from $30,000 to $100,000 or more.

Geographer (IAR) ➡

Geographers study the earth and its interaction with the humans who live on it. Using qualitative methods, such as field observation, and quantitative methods, such as statistical analysis, they gather information about areas of interest, interpret and integrate their findings, and then write reports and give advice. The two major types of geography are physical and human: physical geography includes such topics as climate and plant life; human geography includes such specialties as cultural, political, urban, economic, environmental, and medical geography. Geographers are often employed by the federal government. Other employers include educational institutions and architectural and engineering firms. The median annual wages in 2013 were $74,750.

Historian (IAS) ➡

Historians study and interpret the past. They gather historical data from diverse sources, such as government records, archives, periodicals, photographs, and diaries, evaluating its authenticity and significance. After conducting their own research, they prepare and present their findings and theories. Historians often specialize in a region of the world, a period of time, or a field such as art or music. Historians are employed by governments, educational institutions, businesses, libraries, museums, associations, and historical societies. The median annual wage in 2013 was $55,180.

Instructional Designer (IAE) ➡

Instructional designers analyze instructional and performance problems and suggest interventions for everything from an overall learning strategy to detailed teaching tactics. In addition to determining learning objectives and applying instructional technology, they frequently collaborate with subject matter experts, whose content they organize and format using principles of learning. They may implement their training in a pilot session and then evaluate and revise their instructional material to improve its effectiveness. Instructional designers are hired by corporations, any company that does in-house training, education and training companies, educational institutions, government agencies, training firms, multimedia firms, consulting firms, and professional associations. They may also freelance. The median annual wage in 2013 was $60,610.

Perfumer (IAR) ➡ ■

Perfumers create fragrances. Using a variety of fragrance aromas, trial-and-error experimentation, and previous chemical research, they design fragrance formulas of forty to one hundred ingredients, evaluating them with a trained nose. Perfumers tend to specialize in either fine fragrance (perfumes) or functional fragrance (for shampoo, detergent, and so on). Although some perfumers work for fashion houses, most work for fragrance houses.

Philologist (AIS) ➡

Philologists study the structure and development of a specific language or language group, including such characteristics as morphology, semantics, phonology, accent, and grammar. They trace the origin and evolution of words and syntax, identify and classify obscure languages, and reconstruct and decipher ancient languages. **Etymologists** specialize in the origin, history, and development of words. Philologists are hired by universities and museums, industry, and public agencies. They may also consult to the government.

Political Scientist (IAE) ➡

Political scientists study the development and functioning of political systems. They conduct research on subjects ranging from small-town politics to public policy to international relations. They gather, analyze, and interpret data; prepare their findings for publications and presentations; apply their knowledge to political problems; and may consult with and make recommendations to various organizations. Political scientists are employed by governments, civic groups, research agencies, political parties, educational institutions, and international organizations. The median annual wage in 2013 was $100,920.

Social Psychologist (IAE) ➡

Social psychologists investigate human behavior in a social environment, attempting through research to understand and predict the behavior of individuals in groups. The groups studied may be racial, religious, political, or occupational in nature; the research might focus on such topics as leadership, group dynamics, or romantic attraction. Social psychologists design experiments, collect and analyze data, and present their findings. They work in universities, colleges, marketing-research firms, management consulting firms, and government agencies. The median annual wage in 2013 was $67,760.

Sociologist (IAE) ➡

Sociologists study human society and social groups, including group characteristics and how groups affect individuals as well as other groups. Specialties include racial relations, criminology, and demography. After planning their research, they collect, analyze, and interpret the data and report their findings. They may develop solutions to group problems and consult to businesses, government, and social services. Sociologists are employed by governments, educational institutions, management and public-relations firms, social service agencies, and businesses. The median annual wage in 2013 was $72,430.

COORDINATORS

Advertising Account Executive (AES)

Account executives work in advertising agencies, coordinating advertising campaigns for their clients. After learning from their client about the products or services to be advertised, they draw on their knowledge of the media and the target audience and consult with agency staff to develop an advertising approach and estimate a budget. The account executive then submits the plan and budget to the client and, if it's approved, directs the work of copywriters, layout artists, market researchers, and others who carry out the campaign. The median annual wage for advertising managers in 2013 was $93,880.

Animal Park Program Coordinator (AES)

Program coordinators work in amusement parks that feature performing animals. After gathering educational information and verifying the format of the performance with the animal trainer, they write or review a script to accompany the show. They also prepare brochures, greet visitors, and answer questions. Some program coordinators memorize the script and speak during the performance.

Classification and Treatment Director (EAS)

Classification and treatment directors work in prisons and other correctional institutions, planning, coordinating, and directing rehabilitation programs. Following established guidelines, they provide for the emotional, physical, social, and spiritual needs of inmates. After administering psychological tests and reviewing case reports, they assess an inmate's potential for rehabilitation and recommend a disposition, such as parole, transfer, treatment, or training. They also give speeches to educate the public.

Director of Vital Statistics (EAI)

Directors of vital statistics conduct special statistical studies and direct the activities of subordinates who collect, record, and tabulate statistics on events such as births, deaths, marriages, and diseases. They develop procedures for sampling, collecting, analyzing, and presenting their data; they also develop methods for registering or certifying births and deaths and other events throughout the state. Directors of vital statistics are employed by state governments.

Forms Analysis Manager (EAS)

Forms analysis managers coordinate the analysis of business forms, with the goals of improving format and design, increasing content effectiveness, and reducing production costs. Once their staff has identified problems and recommended solutions, forms analysis managers evaluate their recommendations and approve changes. Forms analysis managers are employed by large companies and federal, state, and county governments.

Instructional Material Director (EAS)

Instructional material directors work for public school districts, coordinating the development and use of educational material. After reviewing educational materials such as textbooks and videos, they recommend the purchase of new material, implement its use in the schools, direct workers who maintain and distribute educational materials, and train teachers to use new technology. They also help staff develop their own instructional materials. The median annual wage for an instructional coordinator in 2013 was $60,610.

Location Manager (EAR)

Location managers find interior and exterior settings and get permits to use property for photographs and movies. After learning from the director about the kinds of background needed for scenes, they seek out locations. Once a suitable location is found, they negotiate to use the property and obtain permission to photograph or film on site. They may hire extras and arrange for transportation of the crew. Location managers are hired by photographers and film producers and directors.

Program Proposals Coordinator (EAS)

Program proposals coordinators work for radio and television broadcasters, developing, writing, submitting, and editing proposals for new radio or TV programs. Based on their knowledge of the station's programming needs and budget, they decide whether proposed programs are feasible. They authorize preparation of budgets and act as liaison between the proposal originators and the program production department. Once a proposal is accepted, they facilitate its development by selecting producers, consultants, researchers, and on-air personalities.

Radio Program Director (EAS)

Program directors work for radio stations, selecting the stations' programs and formats (such as Top 40, classical, country). Sometimes they also act as music directors, selecting the music for specific programs. Program directors decide on the number and timing of news, weather, and public service announcements and develop segues between them. Often they research the market to learn what kind of music their audience wants to hear so that they can adjust their programs and attract more listeners. They may also hire and supervise disc jockeys. The median annual wage in 2013 was $69,480.

Records Analysis Manager (EAI)

Records analysis managers coordinate the analysis of records management systems, with the goals of simplifying filing systems, protecting important records, and reducing waste. Balancing information management principles with budgetary constraints and organizational policy, they evaluate staff recommendations and approve certain changes. Records analysis managers are employed by large companies and county, state, and federal governments.

Reports Analysis Manager (EAS)

Reports analysis managers coordinate the analysis of existing reports to plan new, more cost-effective report formats. They evaluate and approve certain recommendations based on their knowledge of cost-control practices, vital records protection, and organizational policies. Reports analysis managers are employed by large companies and federal, state, and county governments.

School Art Coordinator (EAS)

Art coordinators work for school districts, directing teachers of art and crafts and, with the help of teachers and administrators, developing a curriculum for art education. To improve classroom instruction, they observe and evaluate teachers and make recommendations. They also plan and run teacher-training programs, develop instructional materials, authorize the purchase of art supplies, and organize art shows to represent the schools at community events. In 2013, median annual wages for instructional coordinators were $29.14 hourly and $60,610 annually.

School Music Coordinator (EAS)

Music coordinators work for school districts, directing teachers of vocal and instrumental music and, with the help of teachers and administrators, developing a curriculum for music education. To improve classroom instruction, they observe and evaluate teachers and make recommendations. They also plan and run teacher-training programs, develop instructional materials, authorize the purchase and repair of musical instruments, and organize musical groups to represent the schools at community events. The median annual wage for an instructional coordinator in 2013 was $60,610.

Television Program Director (EAS)

Program directors select and schedule the programming broadcast by their TV stations. To provide a balanced mix of programs that will attract a large audience and high ratings, they consult with marketers, study demographics, and watch programs on competitive stations. Following FCC regulations, they choose film packages, syndicated shows, reruns, and locally produced programs, scheduling them with public service announcements, station breaks, and commercials. They also purchase programs and follow a budget. Program directors are employed by independent commercial stations, network-affiliated stations, and public TV stations. The median annual wage in 2013 was $69,480.

Traffic-Safety Administrator (EAR)

Traffic-safety administrators work for municipal governments, planning and directing traffic-safety programs. They examine the patterns of traffic accidents to determine where improvements need to be made, and they coordinate the activities of volunteer groups dedicated to traffic safety. They also test employees to determine their driving ability and attitude. The median annual wage for a traffic-safety administrator in 2013 was $51,000.

EVALUATORS

Art Appraiser (IAS)

Art appraisers evaluate works of art to assess their value. When judging the authenticity of an art object, they rely on their knowledge of art history, including materials and techniques employed by different artists.

They examine antiques and paintings and other art objects, verify their authenticity, and test for forgeries. Art appraisers usually freelance their services to art museums, auction houses, corporations, and individuals who collect, insure, buy, or sell art. Large museums and auction houses may have appraisers on staff.

Bar Examiner (EAS)

Bar examiners work for state bar associations, testing candidates who wish to practice law. Using the legal code in their jurisdiction, they prepare a written examination that requires candidates to demonstrate their knowledge of the law. After the examinations are completed, bar examiners evaluate candidate performance against accepted standards, announce the names of those who pass, submit them to an oral examination, and recommend that they be permitted to practice law. The median annual wage in 2013 was $65,000.

Broadcast News Analyst (AES)

Broadcast news analysts (news anchors and directors of news, sports, and weather) analyze and interpret information received from various sources to broadcast it from the stations that employ them. They gather and examine noteworthy items, selecting, editing, and organizing information into appropriate formats. Following background study to develop their perspectives, they present the news and introduce prerecorded or live stories. The median annual wage in 2013 was $60,470.

Cryptanalyst (IAE)

Cryptanalysts decode secret messages for military, political, or law enforcement agencies. They use a variety of techniques to break the code, including computers and even chemical analysis, then attempt to corroborate the decoded message against other sources.

Graphologist (ACS)

Graphologists analyze handwriting to evaluate personality. From a sample of handwriting, they observe both overall appearance and minute detail, interpreting their personality findings according to principles of handwriting analysis. Graphologists consult to business and industry, using their skills in a variety of ways: screening job applicants, eliminating criminal suspects, examining questioned documents, and helping identify individuals with emotional troubles. They may also use their skills to entertain.

Intelligence Research Specialist (AEI)

Intelligence research specialists direct research designed to determine the feasibility of different military strategies. After talking with military leaders and other support staff to better understand the problem and proposed solutions, they use research techniques and computer analyses to predict the probable success of each strategy before recommending or discouraging particular strategies. Intelligence research specialists are employed not only by the military but also by other government agencies.

Intelligence Specialist (AES)

Intelligence specialists analyze information on subversive activities in foreign countries. Drawing on their knowledge of an area's culture, geography, economy, and political structure, they evaluate military activities, political conditions, and enemy propaganda, to facilitate counteraction by the home government. Intelligence specialists work for the military and other government agencies.

Patent Agent (EAI)

Patent agents prepare patent applications and file and present them in patent courts and the U.S. Patent and Trademark Office (USTPO). They must be registered with the USTPO, and they cannot present cases in other courts. Patent agents, who usually have significant training in science or engineering, are employed by law firms; universities; any corporation with a patent or intellectual property department; technological start-ups and businesses that plan, acquire, or license products; and any private individual who needs to prepare and prosecute a patent application. The average salary at private firms was $92,250 in 2013.

PROMOTER

Auctioneer (EAS)

Auctioneers work at auction houses or for auction services, selling merchandise such as artwork, cars, machinery, furniture, or livestock. After appraising and sorting the merchandise, they select an article and either give or ask for a starting bid. To encourage buyers and stimulate bidding, they may describe the article and its history; later they close the sale to the highest bidder.

Fashion Coordinator (EAS)

Fashion coordinators supervise activities that are designed to promote new fashions. After they gain information on developing trends by attending fashion shows, interviewing designers, studying industry publications, and visiting garment centers, they share their analysis to provide direction for buyers. They may also unify the look of the line across departments. Fashion coordinators are employed by retail stores, design houses, textile firms, fashion magazines, buying offices, pattern companies, and apparel manufacturers.

Public-Relations Counselor (EAS) ➡

Public-relations (PR) counselors create positive images for entertainers and entertainment businesses. The counselor prepares a publicity campaign for the client, taking into account the client's budget and needs. After gathering information, they look for a slant that will appeal to the media, write press releases, contact the media, and arrange press conferences and special events. PR counselors are employed by performers, public-relations firms, radio stations, nightclubs, concert halls, theaters, dance companies, record companies, and arenas. Some freelance. According to the Bureau of Labor Statistics, the media annual wage in 2010 was $59,150.

Public-Relations Specialist (EAS) ➡

Public-relations (PR) specialists enhance the image of their employer as they provide information through such strategies as fact sheets, publicity releases, convention exhibits, speaking tours, and social media campaigns. They maintain cooperative relationships with representatives from the media and various public groups. They also seek to understand the attitudes and concerns of their client's customers and employees. PR specialists work for a wide variety of employers, including public figures, businesses, special interest groups, nonprofit organizations and health-care organizations, social service and government agencies, sports organizations, educational and financial institutions, and manufacturing firms, as well as for independent PR firms. Some freelance. The median annual wage in 2013 was $54,940.

Sales-Service Promoter (AES)

Sales-service promoters work for any industry, promoting the products or services of their firm. To increase sales and create goodwill, they prepare displays, call on merchants, tour the country, and give speeches at conventions. Some sales-service promoters demonstrate new technological products.

Social Media Consultant (EAS)

Social media consultants provide advice and strategies to help clients achieve their individual or organizational goals via social media. These consultants follow industry trends, research target markets, analyze data from analytic tools, develop campaigns, choose the most appropriate platforms (such as Twitter or LinkedIn), and improve the appearance of web pages. The overall goal is positive online coverage, whether that's measured by better sales, greater exposure, a larger number of followers, or improved consumer engagement. For example, a consultant might purge a Facebook page of embarrassing photos and add a professional headshot with a nicely worded caption to enhance the online image of a client searching for dates or employment. Consultants may also manage crises for their clients. Social media consultants are hired by individuals, political candidates, entrepreneurs, and businesses of all sizes.

COLLECTIONS ORGANIZERS

Acquisitions Librarian (SAI)

Acquisitions librarians choose and order books and periodicals and other materials for a library. After perusing publishers' catalogs and making sure that their preliminary choices do not duplicate those already in the collection, they list publications for purchase and circulate the list within the library for review. They also analyze information on cost and delivery dates to select the best vendor. Acquisitions librarians work in public libraries, academic libraries, special libraries, and government or corporation libraries. The median annual wage for a librarian in 2013 was $55,690.

Archivist (AES)

Archivists identify, appraise, exhibit, and preserve records of historical value. They analyze documents to determine their value to posterity; direct the description, cataloging, and cross-indexing of archival material; and select and edit documents for publication or exhibition. In addition to documents on paper, they may work with photographs, films, videos, sound recordings, and computer records. Archivists may specialize in an area of history or technology or specialize in the type of records they archive. Archivists are employed by federal, state, and local governments; corporations; libraries; museums; historical societies; educational institutions; religious, fraternal, and conservation organizations; hospitals; labor unions; and professional associations. The median annual wage in 2013 was $49,110.

Audiovisual Librarian (EAS)

Audiovisual librarians administer a library of audiovisual materials, such as electronic books, films, cassette tapes, CDs, and framed art prints. They evaluate and purchase materials, summarize new acquisitions for the catalog, help patrons and other library personnel select materials, and plan and conduct audiovisual programs. They may operate audiovisual equipment themselves or train others to operate and maintain it. Audiovisual librarians are employed in academic libraries, public libraries, special libraries, and school libraries and media centers. They may also work in information centers or libraries that are part of the government, corporations, advertising agencies, museums, medical centers, and professional associations. The median annual wage for a librarian in 2013 was $55,690.

Curator (EAI)

Curators oversee and maintain cultural, biological, or historical collections, acquiring new objects and specimens as well as planning and preparing exhibits. They often use computers to catalog, organize, and disseminate information about their collection. Many curators specialize in a field, such as art, botany, history, or paleontology. Curators are employed by museums, zoos, aquariums, botanic gardens, nature centers, and historic sites. The median annual wage in 2013 was $50,550.

Young-Adult and Children's Librarians (AES)

Young-adult and children's librarians provide special services designed to stimulate the reading and communication skills of young adults or children. They acquire books and materials especially suitable for young adults or children, compile lists, give talks, conduct story hour, and help their patrons make selections. After conferring with parents, teachers, and community leaders, they plan and conduct programs and activities, such as creative writing clubs, photography contests, and film series. Young-adult and children's librarians are most likely to work in public libraries and school libraries and media centers. The median annual wage for a librarian in 2013 was $55,690.

LANGUAGE CONVERTERS

Deaf Interpreter (ASC)

Deaf interpreters translate spoken information into visually observed communication for the deaf and hard of hearing. Using gestures, finger spelling, facial expressions, American Sign Language (ASL), cued speech, and other methods, they interpret language between people who can hear and people who are deaf. They may also convert sign language into oral or written language for those who can hear. Some interpreters translate television broadcasts for deaf viewers. Deaf interpreters are employed by educational institutions, broadcasting stations, social service agencies and government agencies, and interpretation companies. In 2013, median annual wages were $45,430.

Foreign Language Interpreter (ASC)

Foreign language interpreters listen to a passage spoken in one language and translate it into another language. Quickly and accurately, they convert meanings to communicate between people who do not share the same language. They typically interpret the information by one of three methods: whispered, consecutive, or simultaneous. Specialties include travel, conference, legal, and health-care interpretation. Foreign language interpreters may be employed by educational and legal institutions, hospitals and other medical centers, conference centers, international businesses, interpretation companies, the military, and government agencies. In 2013, median annual wages were $45,430.

Translator (AIC)

Translators rewrite a text written in one language in order to express the same ideas in a different language. After reading the original text to interpret its meaning, which requires being fluent in the foreign language as well as understanding the language's culture, translators convert the information, maintaining the style and tone of the original source, following rules of grammar and composition in their own language. They work on a computer, receive and submit their work electronically, and use computer-assisted translation (CAT) tools. They may translate legal, scientific, technical, and journalistic texts as well as more literary texts. **Localizers** translate text related to products and services that originated in a place with a different language. Translators may be hired by translation companies, businesses, manufacturing firms, book publishers, the military, and government agencies. Most work from home. In 2013, median annual wages were $45,430.

MODELS

Artist's Model (AES)

Artists' models pose as a subject for painters and sculptors and other visual artists. They may specialize in nude or clothed posing, sometimes providing their own costumes. They are employed by art schools, artists' organizations, and individual artists. The median hourly wage in 2013 was $9.15 per hour or $19,040 annually.

Fashion Model (EAS)

Fashion models try on clothing for customers, buyers, salespeople, and garment designers. Dressing in coats, suits, swimwear, or other garments, they stand, turn, and walk to demonstrate the features of the clothes they wear. Most models find work through agents, in department stores, custom salons, manufacturers' showrooms, fashion shows, and trade shows. The median hourly wage for models in 2013 was $9.15 per hour or $19,040 annually. **Runway models** typically earn a flat fee for one show, starting at about $150 and going into the thousands.

Photographer's Model (AES)

Photographers' models pose for pictures that are used to advertise merchandise. After makeup application and hair styling, they pose as instructed by the photographer or strike their own interpretive poses. Some models specialize in just one part of the body, such as hands, or just one category of merchandise, such as shoes. Photographers' models are typically self-employed, finding work through modeling agencies and occasionally advertising agencies. Some work directly for photographers. Wages vary widely but rates paid through a reputable agency average $150 to $200 per hour.

Path 2
IDEAS AND PEOPLE

MENTORS

Art Therapist (ASI)

Art therapists use art activities to improve the health and well-being of people with illnesses and disabilities. After assessing patient needs and consulting with other health-care staff, they develop a group or individual plan to build self-confidence, increase social interaction, and express feelings through activities such as painting, crafting, or sculpting. Art therapists are employed by hospitals, schools, nursing homes, extended-care facilities, rehabilitation centers, and independent expressive-arts therapy centers. The median annual wage in 2013 was $43,180.

Clergy Member (SAE)

Clergy members conduct religious worship, provide spiritual guidance, and perform a variety of religious rites according to their faith. For example, they may interpret religious doctrine, write and deliver sermons, teach those who seek conversion, oversee educational programs, conduct weddings and funerals, visit the sick, and comfort the bereaved. Many clergy members serve individual congregations as a minister, priest, or rabbi. Others work in hospitals, educational institutions, correctional institutions, the military, and community service agencies. The median annual wage in 2013 was $43,800.

Counselor (SAE)

Counselors help individuals and groups understand and cope with problems that may be personal, social, educational, or vocational in nature. They assess the nature of the client's concerns and facilitate personal growth and problem solving in the context of a helping relationship. Specialties include career, school, genetic, mental health, multicultural, and drug and alcohol counseling. Counselors are employed by educational institutions, correctional institutions, mental-health centers, health-care facilities, health maintenance organizations, and vocational rehabilitation centers. They may also be self-employed. The median annual wage for a general counselor in 2013 was $43,620.

Dance Therapist (ASI)

Dance therapists plan and lead dance and movement activities to improve the physical and mental health of patients. They lead individual and group dance sessions, adapting their programs as patients progress. Dance therapists are employed by schools, correctional facilities, independent expressive-arts therapy centers, and a variety of health-care facilities, including hospitals, mental-health centers, nursing homes, and rehabilitation centers. The median annual wage for a dance/movement therapist in 2013 was $40,000.

Marriage and Family Therapist (SAE)

Marriage and family therapists help individuals, couples, and families. They may focus on the marital relationship, a child's behavioral problems, or the concerns of blended or stepfamilies. With a focus on resolving present problems, they explore family history or patterns of interaction and make suggestions for change. Marriage and family therapists are employed by mental-health centers, employee-assistance programs, and health maintenance organizations. Some are self-employed in private practice and may consult to religious organizations and family businesses. The median annual wage in 2013 was $48,160.

Music Therapist (ASI)

Music therapists use music and musical activities to improve the physical and emotional health of their patients. Working with other health-care professionals, they plan musical activities designed to help patients build confidence, increase social activity, and express feelings. They may teach songs, play musical instruments, and choose background music for their institution. Music therapists work at hospitals, schools, nursing homes, extended-care facilities, correctional facilities, mental-health centers, rehabilitation centers, and expressive-arts therapy centers. The median annual wage in 2013 was $43,180.

Psychotherapist (SAI)

Psychotherapists use therapeutic principles to help clients recover from problems that are psychological in nature. Although they may use expressive-arts techniques such as journaling or psychodrama, they engage primarily in talk therapy. They may work with individuals, groups, or both, and may develop and provide outreach educational programs. Psycho-therapists may be trained in a variety of disciplines, including counseling and clinical psychology, psychiatry, social work, and Jungian analysis. Therapists are employed by educational institutions, hospitals and clinics, correctional facilities, and mental-health centers. Psychotherapists are often self-employed. Median wages in 2013 for counseling and clinical psychologists were $32.58 hourly and $67,760 annually.

Speech-Language Pathologist (SAI)

Speech-language pathologists, also known as speech therapists, diagnose and treat problems involving speech and language. After reviewing an individual's background, they use special instruments and a variety of tests to evaluate problems such as stuttering or slurred speech. They then plan and implement a treatment program, teaching new skills to their clients and monitoring their progress. Speech pathologists work in educational settings; home-health-care agencies; hospitals and doctor's offices; speech, language, and hearing centers; and in solo or group private practice. The median annual wage in 2013 was $70,810.

NEGOTIATORS

Advertising Manager (EAS)

Advertising managers, also known as advertising directors or sales promotion directors, work for any industry, planning and executing the advertising policies of their organization. They meet with department heads to discuss new strategies and accounts; allocate advertising space and airtime among the different departments or products of their organization; direct the work of the advertising department to gather information, compile statistics, and develop and produce advertisements; review and approve advertisements before they are released; and negotiate contracts with the media. The median annual wage in 2013 was $93,880.

Conservation of Resources Commissioner (AES)

Conservation of resources commissioners work for the state government to conserve natural resources and promote their use in the public interest. These commissioners develop conservation programs and set limits on consumption. They negotiate with mining and drilling companies to observe standards and extract resources efficiently. To solve conservation problems related to economic development, they prepare reports and speak with representatives of government, labor, and industry.

Council on Aging Director (EAS)

Directors for the Council on Aging work in local and state government to solve problems of senior citizens. They plan research studies to learn more about age-related problems and then combat those problems with new policies and strategies. They help set up local programs and services for the elderly, coordinate programs with other organizations, and promote their programs and the interests of the aged by delivering speeches, negotiating with community leaders, preparing educational materials for the public, and recommending changes in public policy and legislation.

Historic Sites Supervisor (EAS)

Historic sites supervisors work in the state government, directing people who acquire and preserve natural phenomena and historic sites such as homes and battlefields. After negotiating with property owners, they authorize the acquisition and restoration of historic sites. These supervisors may also help private individuals and civic groups acquire landmarks that are not suitable for state support, direct archeological research in state parks, and direct the preparation of museum exhibits and multimedia exhibits designed to encourage public attendance.

Minister of Music (ASE) ➡

Music ministers work for churches and other religious groups, directing musical programs for large congregations. In addition to directing the work of staff members and volunteers, they may sing solos, chant or read religious texts during services, arrange music, and lead the congregation in singing. They may compose their own music or variations on traditional church music. They may also lead the choir and teach singing or chanting to groups within the congregation. **Cantors** play similar roles in Jewish synagogues.

Newspaper Editor (AES) ➡

Newspaper editors formulate editorial policies and direct the operation of a newspaper. They appoint heads to the advertising, circulation, and production departments and supervise their work. Negotiating with departmental heads and an editorial policy committee, they develop policies and procedures for the paper. Newspaper editors also write editorials, review financial reports, and represent their employing paper at various functions. The median annual wage in 2013 was $54,150.

Talent Director (EAS)

Talent directors, also known as casting directors or casting agents, audition and select performers for dramatic productions. After reading the script and conferring with the producer of a TV, radio, film, or stage show, talent directors review information about performers and suggest candidates for various roles. They may interview and audition performers, as well as approve their selection and negotiate their contracts. Often hired by producers, talent directors work for theater companies, film and TV production companies, and radio and TV broadcasting companies. In 2013, the median annual wage was $69,480.

Technical and Scientific Publications Editor (ASE) ➡

Editors for technical and scientific publications coordinate the work of writers who prepare material on specific fields, such as manufacturing or medical research. To develop a focus for their publication, they stay abreast of developments and analyze trends. They assign subjects to staff writers, supervise their work, and edit their drafts. Technical and scientific publications editors work in business and industry and for educational institutions, research organizations, nonprofit organizations, and the government. The median annual wage for a general editor in 2013 was $54,150.

Travel Guide (EAS)

Travel guides organize and lead long-distance trips for individuals and groups. Using their knowledge of travel routes and destinations, they plan itineraries for tours, cruises, and expeditions and arrange for accommodations and transportation. In addition to conducting tours and describing points of interest, they may also provide advice on shopping and sightseeing, attend to customers with special needs, and resolve disputes. Travel guides are employed by travel agencies, travel planners, and tour operators. Median wages in 2013 were $16.26 hourly and $33,820 annually.

INSTRUCTORS

Art Teacher (ASE) ➡ ■

Art teachers teach skills such as painting, designing, or sculpturing and may specialize in teaching a particular field such as art history, graphic design, or illustration. After preparing lesson plans and selecting textbooks and supplies, they demonstrate artistic techniques, observe and evaluate their students' work, and provide feedback. Art teachers may also arrange field trips, organize student contests, or plan art exhibits. Art teachers are employed by educational institutions, correctional facilities, and community agencies. They also teach private lessons to individuals and offer workshops through guilds and other organizations. The median annual wage for elementary school teachers in 2013 was $53,590; for secondary school teachers, $55,360.

Child-Care Attendant (SAE)

Child-care attendants help prekindergarten children, organizing and leading activities in daycare centers, preschools, and playrooms. They read to children, set up art projects, teach games and songs, and help children develop habits of self-care. They also maintain discipline, serve meals, and monitor rest periods. Child-care attendants work in nursery schools, preschools, child daycare centers, and playrooms provided by organizations such as universities, theaters, department stores, hotels, and historic sites. In 2013, child-care workers earned median wages of $9.42 hourly and $19,600 annually.

Choreographer (AES) ➡

Choreographers compose original dances or new interpretations of traditional dance music. After studying the music and any script involved, they create dance routines and block the movements out on stage, adapting the choreography as needed once rehearsal begins. They may audition performers, choose dancers for the cast, and teach them the dance steps and routines during rehearsal. Choreographers may specialize in different dance forms, such as ballet, jazz, folk, or modern dance. Choreographers are hired, usually one show at a time, by producers of shows for theaters and nightclubs or by producers of shows for TV or film. The median annual wage in 2013 was $44,130.

Coach (ASE)

Coaches help clients improve their functioning in different areas: for example, online dating coaches help clients attract a trustworthy mate; writing coaches help clients produce quality written work; voice coaches help with improvement of the speaking or singing voice; dramatic coaches help actors and actresses improve their acting techniques. After evaluating a client's ability, they teach skills and offer advice. Many coaches work independently; some coaches, such as dramatic coaches, may be employed by schools, colleges, universities, and theater groups. The median annual wage for a general coach in 2013 was $29,150.

Dancing Instructor (ASE) ➡

Dancing instructors plan lessons after observing their students' abilities and limitations. Explaining and demonstrating dancing styles, techniques, and steps, they give feedback as students practice new skills.

They may specialize in teaching one or more forms of dance, such as ballet, jazz, tap, modern, or ballroom dance. Dancing instructors are employed by private schools, educational institutions, and dance studios. The median annual wage in 2013 was $38,000.

Drama Teacher (ASE) ➡

Drama teachers teach acting and other theater arts and may produce and direct plays. They evaluate the abilities and limitations of their students and plan instruction. Using lecture, demonstration, improvisation, and other exercises, they teach dramatic principles and techniques such as character development, dialect, movement, and projection. They may audition students, assign roles, direct rehearsals, and supervise nonperformance tasks such as constructing the set, operating the lights, designing the costumes, or applying stage makeup. Drama teachers are usually employed by educational institutions. The median annual wage in 2013 for secondary school teachers was $55,360.

Elementary School Teacher (SAI)

Elementary school teachers work in public and private schools teaching academic subjects, study skills, and rules of social conduct to their students. Sometimes they tutor individual students and meet with parents. The median annual wage in 2013 was $53,590.

English as a Second Language (ESL) Instructor (SAE)

Instructors of English as a Second Language (ESL) teach English as a second language to students who speak a foreign language. They teach basic English skills, including listening, speaking, reading, and writing. They may specialize in skills specific to certain situations, such as shopping or job hunting. They may teach individuals or groups of students at any age from elementary school to adult. ESL instructors are usually self-employed or employed by educational institutions. The median annual salary in 2013 was $47,000 for full-time ESL teachers. However, many ESL instructors work on a part-time basis, and wages vary greatly from region to region.

Graduate Assistant (SAE)

Although no one would really aspire to a career as a graduate assistant per se, this is a way to support yourself as you prepare for a career that requires graduate study. Graduate assistants help faculty in colleges and universities teach courses and do research. For example, graduate assistants may teach lower-level courses, grade papers and exams, facilitate discussion in study sections, do library or laboratory research, prepare data for statistical analysis, and write up research results. Graduate assistants are employed by colleges and universities, usually on a part-time basis while taking graduate courses.

Liberal Arts Faculty (SAI)

Liberal arts faculty work for universities, colleges, and community colleges, teaching liberal arts subjects such as fine arts, English literature, foreign languages, and film studies. They prepare and give lectures, facilitate discussion in seminars, give exams and grade papers, and advise students on their course of study. Liberal arts faculty members often do original research in their fields, reading and writing scholarly articles or textbooks. In 2013, the median annual wage was $60,920 for postsecondary English teachers and $62,830 for postsecondary art, drama, and music teachers.

Librarian (SAI)

Librarians help people access information from a collection of books, periodicals, documents, and other materials. They search for information for patrons and also teach patrons how to use reference sources. In addition to maintaining and displaying the library collection, they may also select, order, catalog, classify, and compile lists of library materials.

Librarians may specialize in such areas as reference, outreach, or circulation. Librarians work in academic libraries, public libraries, special libraries, and school libraries and media centers. Librarians may also work in libraries or information centers in the government, religious organizations, medical centers, research laboratories, corporations, law firms, advertising agencies, museums, nonprofit organizations, and professional associations. The median annual wage in 2013 was $55,690.

Modeling Instructor (ASE)

Modeling instructors teach students how to improve their appearance. After observing and analyzing physical characteristics such as figure, posture, and coloring, the instructor explains and demonstrates ways to improve appearance. Incorporating principles of modeling, they teach students how to apply makeup, how to walk and climb stairs, and how to select and coordinate clothing. Modeling instructors are employed by modeling schools and occasionally by modeling agencies.

Music Teacher (AES) ➡ ■

Music teachers teach instrumental music and voice to both individuals and groups, including instruction in such subjects as music appreciation, music theory, and composition. They evaluate the personality and aptitude of an individual student when choosing a beginning instrument and prepare and teach lessons that include demonstration of musical skills and critiques of performance. Music teachers conduct rehearsals, coach individuals, and lead groups in public performance. They may also meet with parents, arrange field trips, and store musical instruments and supplies. Music teachers are employed by educational institutions, including schools, universities, and conservatories. Some work for theaters. Many are self-employed. The median annual wage in 2013 for elementary school music teachers was $62,830.

Preschool Teacher (SAE)

Preschool teachers nurture and teach children under the age of five. In an informal and relatively unstructured setting, they care for the basic needs of small children while they help them learn through play. In addition to organizing activities that will stimulate growth, they see to it that children have time to rest. They also discuss child development with parents. Preschool teachers are employed by families, daycare centers, preschools, religious and educational institutions, the government, businesses, and community agencies. Median wages in 2013 were $13.26 hourly and $27,570 annually.

Secondary School Teacher (SAE)

Secondary school teachers teach one or several subjects—such as English, foreign languages, social studies, speech, and science—to junior high or high school students. They may also meet with parents, sponsor extracurricular activities, and counsel troubled students. Secondary school teachers are employed by public and private high schools and junior high or middle schools. The median annual wage in 2013 was $55,360.

Trainer (SAE)

Trainers develop and conduct training programs for employees, which may include lectures, computer tutorials, storytelling sessions, or multimedia presentations. They conduct training sessions and later evaluate or test trainees to determine the effectiveness of their programs. Trainers may specialize in areas such as career development, writing skills, sales techniques, or cross-cultural aspects of foreign trade. Trainers are employed by corporations, businesses, government agencies, educational and medical institutions, and nonprofit organizations. Self-employed trainers may conduct seminars outside the workplace. The median annual wage in 2013 was $56,850.

SUPERVISORS

Advertising Production Manager (EAS)

Advertising production managers supervise people who prepare advertisements, including designers, illustrators, photographers, and typographers. Visual-technical experts, they review proofs to be sure they meet specifications and coordinate workers to prepare final layouts on schedule. Before submitting final layouts for printing, they examine the layout proof and specify margin widths and color corrections. Advertising production managers work for advertising agencies, printing companies, and in-house corporate marketing departments. Median annual wages for managers in advertising positions in 2013 were $93,880.

City Editor (AES) ➡

City editors work for newspapers, supervising staff that gather and report the news. They direct reporters and photographers to cover developing news events and other stories. They supervise editors, review edited copy, and allocate newspaper space. They may guide the newspaper on policy and position. Median wages for city editors in 2013 were $26.04 hourly and $54,150 annually.

Department Editor (AES) ➡

Department editors work for newspapers, supervising staff on a specialized section of a newspaper, such as sports, business, or entertainment. They select material, assign staff to write or photograph stories, determine content, edit copy, and supervise layout on their section. Department editors may write a regular column as well. Median wages for editors in 2013 were $26.04 hourly and $54,150 annually.

Properties Supervisor (EAS)

Properties supervisors work for producers of motion pictures, supervising and coordinating the work of employees who obtain, move, and fabricate props. After reading the script and talking with the director to determine the props required for each scene, they assign workers to buy, rent, order, or otherwise create props. Properties supervisors have responsibility for the placement of props on the set and for their safekeeping and storage.

Publications Editor (AES) ➡

Publications editors plan the contents of magazines and other publications and supervise their preparation. They choose themes; assign articles to writers, pictures to photographers, and illustrations to artists; write, rewrite, and edit manuscripts; and oversee final production of the publication, including page layouts. Publications editors also hire staff, supervise subordinate editors, negotiate with freelancers, and plan budgets and future issues. Publications editors are employed by magazines and business and trade publishers. Median wages for editors in 2013 were $26.04 hourly and $54,150 annually.

Show Operations Supervisor (ASE)

Show operations supervisors work at amusement parks and theme parks, supervising performers and technicians. With anticipated audience size in mind, they review and adjust the performance schedule and arrange shift assignments. They also answer questions and handle complaints from park guests.

Story Editor (ASE) ➡

Story editors evaluate manuscripts and supervise writers who create scripts for TV and film. They evaluate a story's potential for development into a script and recommend the purchase of material. They hire and assign writers and then review and edit their work to prepare scripts for production. They may work closely with a screenwriter in developing and improving a story. For a reality television show, they may also write dialogue and produce and edit footage. Story editors are employed at TV and film studios and at the larger independent film production companies.

ENTERTAINERS

Amusement Park Entertainer (AES)

Amusement park entertainers entertain their audience by performing a specialty act such as fire eating, snake charming, sword swallowing, organ grinding, or juggling. Amusement park entertainers find work in amusement parks, nightclubs, and live variety shows.

Character Impersonator (EAS)

Character impersonators dress up in costumes and impersonate holiday characters such as the Easter Bunny, storybook characters such Snow White, cartoon characters such as Mickey Mouse, dramatic characters such as Columbo, or celebrities such as Marilyn Monroe. They may talk with parents and children, hand out gifts or samples, ask for donations, pose for pictures, take part in parades, or demonstrate something for sale. Character impersonators may be hired to promote sales at retail stores, conventions, or exhibits; to enhance corporate parties; or to amuse children at restaurants, hospitals, or amusement parks.

Psychic Reader (AEC)

Psychic readers entertain an audience by using psychic abilities to tell about past or future events. They may gaze into crystal balls, tell fortunes, or read palms, cards, or tea leaves. Psychic readers may work for hotlines or find work through entertainment agencies. Some volunteer their services at police departments; some work at fairs or carnivals. Self-employed psychics develop a private clientele, sometimes selling their services through 900-number lines.

Singing Messenger (ASC)

Singing messengers work for message-delivery services, singing and dancing while they deliver messages to individuals. After learning song and dance routines, they take a customer's message, dress up in makeup and costume if necessary, travel to the recipient of the message, and perform the routine. They may play a musical instrument during the performance or deliver a gift afterward.

PERSUADERS

Apparel and Accessories Salesperson (EAS)

Apparel salespeople sell men's, women's, and children's clothing, as well as accessories such as hats and shoes. They advise customers on fashion and fit, make out sales slips, take payment, give change, and put merchandise on racks and in bags. Clothing and accessories salespeople work in department stores, clothing stores, boutiques, shoe stores, sporting goods stores, and specialty shops. Median hourly wages in 2013 were $10.16 in clothing and department stores.

Dancing Instruction Sales Representative (EAS)

Dance studios hire sales representatives to sell dancing instructions. After interviewing and dancing with patrons to learn about their background and skills, the sales rep discusses their dancing ability, proposes a teaching plan, and persuades them to buy lessons. Sales reps may also prepare a contract and receive payment. Some sales reps are also dancing instructors.

Fabric Salesperson (EAS)

Fabric salespeople sell fabrics and sewing accessories. They discuss features, suggest complementary fabrics, and measure and cut the required length of goods from the bolt. They also display a variety of material and notions, give customers advice, operate the cash register, and figure costs. Fabric salespeople work in fabric stores, department stores, and stores that specialize in drapery and upholstery material. The median hourly wage in 2013 was $10.16 in general merchandise stores.

Flower Salesperson (EAR)

Flower salespeople work at retail florist shops, selling fresh and artificial flowers, potted plants, vases, and other accessories. They display flowers in the store and give advice to customers about flowers and arrangements for special occasions. In addition to handling payment and delivery, they may design and assemble corsages and bouquets and other floral arrangements.

Graphic Art Sales Representative (EAS)

Graphic art sales reps sell the work of illustrators, photographers, and graphic artists to advertising agencies, in-house advertising departments, and collateral designers. They compose and sketch a layout, give examples of available artwork, compute the cost of the job, and later deliver an advertisement or illustration. The median annual wage for an advertising sales representative in 2013 was $45,830. Many sales positions also offer commissions in addition to a base salary.

Wedding Consultant (AES)

Wedding consultants provide advice and help plan and personalize all aspects of a wedding. Not all wedding consultants provide the same services, but most offer some of the following: maintaining a gift register and selling wedding gifts; selling wedding gowns and making recommendations regarding the bridal trousseau and clothing for the bridal party; shopping for the bride or helping her choose china, silverware, glassware, flowers, and the like; arranging for music and photography and a catering service; and providing advice on etiquette during rehearsal. Wedding consultants are usually self-employed, charging either a flat fee or about 10 percent of the total wedding cost; others charge from $50 to $150 per hour. Some work in bridal shops and large department stores. The median annual salary for general event planners in 2013 was $46,260.

Path 3
IDEAS AND THINGS

DESIGNERS

Architect (AIR) ➡

Architects plan and design buildings. Using their knowledge of design, engineering, building materials, building codes, and construction methods, they design a plan to meet a particular client's needs, prepare scale drawings and specifications, and draw up building contracts. Architects may help their clients get bids and select contractors; periodically they may observe on-site construction. Specialties include commercial, residential, industrial, marine, and institutional architecture. Architects work for architecture firms, engineering firms, schools of architecture, builders, real estate developers, industrial organizations, the military, and government agencies. The median annual wage in 2013 was $74,110.

Art Director (AES) ➡

Art directors design and direct the construction of sets for motion pictures and television productions. After reading the script and conferring with the producer and director, they research appropriate architectural styles, estimate construction costs, present plans and estimates, and coordinate the construction and decoration of the set to ensure that it follows their design. Art directors also direct the production of graphics and animation. They are hired by TV and film directors and production designers. The median annual salary for art directors in stage, motion pictures, and television in 2013 was $69,480.

Bank-Note Designer (AER) ➡

Bank-note designers design currency, stamps, bonds, and other securities for governments. They modify original sketches as needed, given technical constraints; draw new design elements to discourage counterfeiting; and select or suggest ink colors. They may originate new designs and get approval from the issuing agency. **Sculptor-engravers** design coins and medals for governments.

Cloth Designer (AER) ➡

Cloth designers, also known as textile designers, create new designs for textiles, including rugs and woven fabrics. Combining their knowledge of textiles with information on fashion trends, they design new fabric, specifying such details as color, pattern, and finish. They sketch their designs and examine a sample of fabric to see if further modifications are needed. Cloth designers are employed by manufacturers of textiles, apparel, linens, and upholstery fabric.

Color Expert (AES) ➡

Color experts give advice on aesthetic color combinations. They know what shades of color are fashionable and what psychological effects are produced by different colors, and they help their clients choose colors for interiors, fashions, and graphic arts. Color experts are hired by color associations, the fashion and textile industries, and architectural, interior design, and graphic design firms.

Display Designer (AES) ➡

Display designers design banners, flags, and other decorations for special occasions and corporate events. After talking with clients about the celebration, theme, and budget, they sketch a design, select decorations or construct new decorations, and may direct others to construct and set up decorations. Display artists design interior displays, window displays, and trade show booths; outside display designers specialize in designing outdoor displays. Display designers are employed by graphic design firms, department stores, and display houses.

Exhibit Designer (ASE) ➡

Exhibit designers work for museums, designing both permanent and temporary exhibits and displays. They confer with museum administrators and staff to learn the exhibit's purpose, content, location, and budget. They then plan the construction of the exhibit, preparing preliminary drawings and detailed construction diagrams. Exhibit designers submit the design for approval and adapt it as needed; oversee construction and installation of the exhibit to ensure that it conforms to their specifications; and arrange for acquisition and placement of objects in the exhibit, along with accompanying information. The median annual salary in 2013 was $50,000.

Facility Planner (AIE) ➡

Facility planners develop plans for how best to utilize the work space of large employers. They analyze the needs of their clients and recommend the best way to lay out office space and other spaces. For long-range plans, they may work with architects in the early stages. Facility planners are employed by architectural or interior design firms, large corporations, government agencies, educational institutions, medical centers, shopping malls, prisons, and utility companies.

Fashion Designer (ASR) ➡

Fashion designers create new designs for men's, women's, and children's clothing and accessories. After analyzing fashion trends, they sketch drawings of their design, examine the sample on a model, and alter the design if necessary. Clothes designers may specialize according to the kind of clothes they design, such as sportswear or accessories. Fashion designers are employed by clothing and pattern manufacturers, fashion salons, high-fashion department stores, and specialty shops. Some freelance, doing custom work for individuals. Costume designers work for theater companies, dance ensembles, and directors and producers of movies and TV shows. The median annual wage in 2013 was $63,760.

Floral Designer (RAE) ➡

Floral designers work for florists, selecting and arranging flowers and other foliage according to customer request. They talk with the customer about the occasion, the kind of arrangement desired, and price and delivery details. To create the arrangement, they use living, dried, or artificial plant material and a variety of tools, such as foam, trimmers, wire, and floral tape. The median annual wage in 2013 was $24,220.

Fur Designer (ACS) ➡

Fur designers design garments made of fur for individual customers or the commercial fur apparel industry. They sketch a design, take customer measurements, draw a pattern, and cut canvas to construct a mock garment. After checking the fit and making alterations, they direct those who sew the fur and then examine the finished product. Fur designers may also redesign fur garments and estimate the costs involved in making new or restyled fur fashions.

Furniture Designer (AES) ➡

Furniture designers work for furniture manufacturers, designing furniture and fixtures (fixtures are furniture that doesn't move, such as display cases). After studying the market, brainstorming, and considering production feasibility, they sketch an article of furniture. If approved, they draw a to-scale original, prepare an itemized list of production requirements, help prepare blueprints, and specify the kinds of material to be used in building the article. They may build models or direct others to build models. In 2013, the median annual wage for designers in a variety of specialties was $62,370.

Graphic Designer (AER) ➡

Graphic designers are visual communicators. They choose visual elements—such as illustrations or photographs or electronic images—and design them for commercial purposes. Graphic designers may design printed materials, such as annual reports or company logos. They may also create images that are projected or generated in other media, such as a series of cartoon scenes used to guide the visual part of producing a commercial. Graphic designers are employed by newspapers, book and magazine publishers, TV and film studios, retail stores, design studios, advertising agencies, public-relations firms, greeting card companies, websites, and corporate advertising departments. Earnings of freelance graphic designers can vary widely based on a wide variety of factors. For graphic designers who work in-house, the annual median wage in 2013 was $44,830.

Greeting Card Designer (AER) ➡

Greeting card designers create the visual and tactile cards that carry the words of a greeting or sentiment. They bring together the talents of illustrators, graphic designers, photographers, and cartoonists. They may be employed by a large greeting card company or freelance to several companies.

Human Factors Designer (IAR) ➡

Human factors designers, also known as ergonomists, design products and systems to make them easier and safer for people to use. To reduce human error and improve comfort and satisfaction, they research how people use products, such as airplane cockpits or kitchen utensils, or systems like those for transporting people or communicating information. Typically, they collaborate with a team that includes industrial designers, engineers, safety experts, and production workers. Human factors designers work for manufacturing companies, research firms, and consulting firms. The median annual wage in 2013 was $80,300.

Industrial Designer (AES) ➡

Industrial designers, also known as commercial designers or product designers, design physical objects for mass markets such as vehicles, toys, appliances, and other equipment. They research products, generate and evaluate design ideas based on practical and aesthetic considerations, and develop designs that are functional, visually appealing, and competitive. They sketch and present their designs, modifying them after discussion. Industrial designers are employed by consulting firms and large manufacturing companies. The median annual wage for commercial and industrial designers in 2013 was $62,370.

Interior Designer (ASE) ➡

Interior designers plan, design, and furnish interior space in many different kinds of buildings, both public and private. Combining client budget and preferences with interior design principles, they design space that is functional and aesthetically pleasing. They draw and illustrate their plans for the client, including specifications for furnishings and lighting; advise clients about color and layout; and may select furnishings, floor coverings, curtains, and accessories. Interior designers are employed by architectural or interior design firms, department stores and home furnishings stores, corporations, furniture and textile manufacturers, design magazines, and hotel, restaurant, and theater chains. Many are self-employed. The median annual wage in 2013 was $48,500.

Inventor (AIR) ➡

Inventors devise new processes or products based on their innovative ideas. Most inventors are employed by in-house research and development departments in technical and scientific organizations such as the automotive, electronic, and pharmaceutical industries. The major exception to this is toy and game inventors, who tend to freelance. Many professional inventors are first trained as industrial designers. The emergence of new technologies, such as 3-D design and printing capabilities, is leading to an ever-growing overlap between the creative and technical aspects of invention and innovation.

Landscape Architect (AIR) ➡

Landscape architects design parks; golf courses; commercial, industrial, and residential sites; and other land development projects. They work with engineers and architects to serve organizations such as municipalities or real estate development firms. To begin, they gather and analyze information from a site, such as soil condition, water drainage, sun exposure, established vegetation, and already existing facilities. They then prepare plans for the site that integrate new facilities and foliage. Once approved, they draw up detailed plans, methods of construction, and lists of materials. Landscape architects are employed by architectural firms and firms that provide landscape architecture services. Some work for federal, state, and local governments, and some are self-employed. The median annual wage in 2013 was $64,790.

Lighting Designer (AER) ➡

Lighting designers select and arrange lighting to set the mood for performance events. First they study working drawings of the stage, read the script, and consult with the show's director and scenic designer. They then design a lighting plan that incorporates lights, filters, and colors to illuminate the action and create specific effects such as a moonlit night or a foggy day. They may be electricians who install the lighting themselves, or they may direct an electrical crew. Lighting designers are employed by universities, colleges, regional theaters, and production companies. They may also freelance to rock bands, performance artists, and dance troupes. Audio and video equipment technicians may also design and operate custom lighting systems. The annual median wage for audio and video equipment technicians in 2013 was $41,250.

Memorial Designer (AER) ➡

Memorial designers design the stonework used in cemeteries, including monuments and statues. After consulting with clients to learn their preferences, they design a memorial and carve their design into a plaster model. The model and specifications are then passed on to a stone carver. Memorial designers may also plan family plots and build models of cemeteries. Memorial designers are employed by memorial studios, monument companies, and the larger quarries and fabricators of granite.

Merchandise Displayer (ARE) ➡

Merchandise displayers work in retail stores, displaying merchandise in windows and on sales floors. They design original displays or follow the manager's suggestions to attract customers to merchandise such as furniture or clothing or cooking equipment. Using hand tools and a variety of materials, they construct backgrounds and props on which they arrange merchandise and place signs. Some merchandise displayers are employed by display houses that produce displays for showrooms, trade shows, and special events.

Movie and Television Set Designers (AIE) ➡

These designers design sets for movies as well as for television. After consulting the art director, they complete the set design, prepare scale construction drawings, and adapt as needed. **Miniature set designers** design miniature sets that are used as background and for special effects. Set designers find work through art directors or production designers. The median annual wage for a set designer in 2013 was $50,000.

Musical Instrument Designer (ARE) ➡

Musical instrument designers build instruments such as violins, guitars, and flutes. After examining related instruments, they craft wood and metal and other materials into functioning instruments. Some builders construct custom-designed instruments for classical musicians or rock stars. Musical instrument designers are employed by music factories and stores; some are self-employed in their own shops.

Ornamental Metalwork Designer (ARS) ➡

Ornamental metalwork designers design ornamental metal items, such as grills, latticework, statuary, railings, and light fixtures. Combining information about the setting, properties of metal, principles of design, and fabrication techniques, they create a design according to customer specifications. They forge tools, draw detailed sketches, and prescribe the techniques to be used. Ornamental metalwork designers are employed by ornamental design shops and iron fabricators, as well as architectural firms, interior design firms, and engineering firms. Some are self-employed.

Package Designer (AEI) ➡

Package designers design containers for products like food, cosmetics, and drugs. After learning about the market and practical requirements for packaging, they create designs that will attract customers and be relatively simple to produce, convenient to store and handle, and easy to identify. Usually they build models and make changes as necessary. Package designers are employed by package design firms, graphic design studios, advertising agencies, and corporations. The median annual wage for commercial designers in 2013 was $62,370.

Safety-Clothing-and-Equipment Designer (AER) ➡

Safety-clothing-and-equipment designers work for manufacturers of protective gear, designing clothing and equipment to protect workers in hazardous conditions. After researching hazardous conditions (such as fire or toxic fumes), they design suits and helmets that might include protective devices (such as mechanical breathing apparatus or communication systems), draft full-scale pattern parts on paper, and tell employees how to cut and construct a sample item.

Set Decorator (AES) ➡

Set decorators decorate sets for movies and TV shows. They read the scripts and choose decorations such as lamps, rugs, window treatments, and furniture. They direct assistants to place decorations on the set and make sure that the dressed set will not interfere with the movements of the cast or the vision of the camera crew. Set decorators find work through film and TV art directors.

Sound Designer (ARE)

Sound designers create the sounds that help set the mood for a stage production. They enhance the action by selecting and integrating live or prerecorded sounds that may be musical, unrecognizable, or realistic, such as doorbells or thunder or gunshots. The median annual wage for a sound designer in 2013 was $46,480.

Theater Set Designer (AES) ➡

These designers design sets for theater companies. They learn from the director the requirements for the set and research the appropriate style for the work to be performed. Keeping budget and scene changes in mind, they draw a design, indicating floor plans, scenery, borders, and props. In addition to directing the building of the set, they may also build models to scale and design the lighting. The median annual wage for a set designer in 2013 was $50,000.

Urban Designer (AIR)

Urban designers are responsible for the look and feel of communities and urban areas. Most often trained in architecture, they are employed by city governments to implement balanced plans for urban landscapes. Projects might include additions, such as new sports complexes or shopping malls, and revisions of existing areas, such as harbors and inner cities. Based on whether construction proposals would enhance or detract from the beauty and function of the community, urban designers decide whether or not to approve them. The median annual wage for urban and regional planners in 2013 was $65,650.

IMAGE MAKERS

Animator (ARI) ➡

Animators use traditional animation techniques and computer technology to create film or video products containing images that are not derived from live-action photographs. A kindred industry is digital visual effects. Both the animation and visual effects industries comprise six artistic occupational families: visual development, story, layout, painting, traditional animation, and computer. Animators may work for film or TV studios, new media companies, or independent production houses. The median annual wage in 2013 was $64,470.

Bonsai Culturist (RAE)

Bonsai culturists grow dwarf trees. After selecting small trees that are suitable for bonsai, they prune roots and branches and add chemicals to the soil to stunt growth. Using cutters and wires, they train tree limbs to create artistic forms. They choose aesthetically pleasing containers in which to plant their trees and arrange moss and rocks and other decorations around them. Bonsai culturists are employed by bonsai nurseries, organizations that collect or exhibit bonsai, and landscape designers who showcase bonsai gardens.

Cartoonist (AES) ➡

Cartoonists draw cartoons for print media. After developing their ideas, they sketch a cartoon, get feedback, and make changes. Some cartoonists write their own captions, using talents with humor or criticism. Specialties include comic strips and sports or editorial cartoons. Cartoonists are hired by newspapers, magazines, news services, and advertising agencies.

Continuity Artist (ASE)

Continuity artists sketch possible scenes from TV and film scripts, to help directors envision the sequence of images. Their sketches, numbering over a thousand for an average film, help to develop the sequence of scenes and may also set the overall mood for the production. Continuity artists are employed by producers and directors of film, TV, and multimedia.

Crafter (RAC)

Crafters create artistic objects, either functional or decorative, by hand. After developing an idea and perhaps creating a prototype, they select materials such as fiber, metal, wax, glass, or wood and assemble them with tools. Some traditional crafts include pottery, jewelry, basketry, weaving, and quilting. Crafters may be employed by studios, but most work independently and sell through galleries and craft shows. Median wages for craft artists in 2013 were $14.62 hourly and $30,400 annually.

Fashion Artist (AEI)

Fashion artists draw illustrations of clothing and accessories for advertisements. They position the item to accentuate its desirable features and then draw or paint it, often including figures and other background. They may also draw lettering. Fashion artists are employed by department stores, mail-order catalogs, newspapers, magazines, and fashion advertising agencies.

Illustrator (AER) ➡

Illustrators paint or draw pictures to illustrate words in such diverse products as books, magazines, greeting cards, calendars, stationery, and wrapping paper. They draw illustrations, seek feedback, and make changes. Some illustrators specialize in title art, and paint or draw the lettering used in titles and commercial logos. Illustrators are employed by book, magazine, and greeting card publishers; film, video, and paper products producers; and advertising agencies. The median annual wage for fine artists in 2013 was $42,610.

Makeup Artist (AER) ➡

Makeup artists apply makeup to stage and film performers so that their appearance, including facial features, skin texture, and body shape, is appropriate for their roles. To create an image of the character, they study sketches and photographs and plaster models in period files. They confer with performers and managers about production requirements, order cosmetics and supplies, and design and apply prostheses. Makeup artists are hired by costume designers, theater groups, and makeup companies. They may freelance their services to models, photographers, beauty salons, department stores, advertising agencies, private clients, fashion shows, and TV or film production companies. Median wages for performance and theatrical makeup artists in 2013 were $22.70 hourly and $47,210 annually.

Medical and Scientific Illustrator (AIE) ➡

Medical and scientific illustrators create drawings, diagrams, and three-dimensional models of subjects including pathology, medical procedures, parts of the body, and plant and animal tissue. Their illustrations are done in a variety of media, including pen and ink, watercolor, plastics, and plaster. Their illustrations are used in teaching, research, publications, exhibits, and consultation. **Histological illustrators** specialize in drawing plant and animal tissue. Medical and scientific illustrators are employed by medical centers, teaching institutions, and publishers of medical and scientific information, including journals and textbooks. Many are self-employed and may freelance to doctors and lawyers who need exhibits for court cases. According to the Association of Medical Illustrators, annual wages range from $61,000 to $150,000. They also report that approximately 46 percent of salaried illustrators supplement their income with freelance work.

Painter (ASI) ➡

Painters paint original compositions such as landscapes, still lifes, and portraits. Painters are usually self-employed, selling their work to individual art collectors and to stores, museums, and art galleries. They may also do murals and other large decorative work for businesses and local community groups, as well as airbrush work on vehicles, T-shirts, and other media. The median annual wage for fine artists in 2013 was $42,610.

Pewterer (ARS) ➡

Pewterers design new merchandise for manufacturers of pewter products. Using their knowledge of metallurgy and mold making, they fabricate models of new casting molds, mix and heat alloy, fill casting molds, and finish the product using a variety of tools such as lathes and blowtorches. To facilitate the finishing process, they adapt tools and fabricate lathe accessories as needed.

Police Artist (ASC) ➡

Police artists work for law enforcement agencies, sketching crime scenes and likenesses of criminal suspects. To draw a suspected criminal, they question victims and witnesses about the suspect's body type, facial features, and other identifying characteristics and then sketch a series of simple line drawings that fit the descriptions. They may work from photographs or sketch on site to prepare schematic drawings of the scene of the crime.

Printmaker (AES) ➡

Printmakers conceive and develop printed images for designs that they etch, engrave, or carve into material such as wood or stone or metal. They choose a printmaking method, render the drawing, ink the surface, and transfer the image to paper or other textured surface. Some printmakers use computer-driven data to create ink-jet prints. Printmakers are employed by printmaking studios and sell their work to collectors and art galleries and museums.

Quick-Sketch Artist (ASE) ➡

Quick-sketch artists draw likenesses of their customers. After posing their customers to highlight appealing features, they use pencil, charcoal, or pastels to draw a quick picture. Some artists work from photographs. **Caricaturists** draw only exaggerated likenesses. Quick-sketch artists are self-employed, usually working in tourist spots or arts festivals.

Sculptor (AER) ➡

Sculptors create three-dimensional works of art from materials such as stone, concrete, wood, or metal, using tools such as chisels, mallets, abrasives, and soldering irons. They may carve their forms from a block of marble, model wax forms and cast them in bronze, model clay forms and fire them in kilns, or arrange and fasten together various man-made and natural materials. Sculptors may get public commissions. They sell their work to individual collectors and those who request private portraits as well as to art galleries, stores, and museums. The median annual wage for fine artists in 2013 was $42,610.

Set Illustrator (AES) ➡

Set illustrators create the backdrop for movies and TV programs and commercials. They read the script, do background research, consult with the art director while developing their plans, and then illustrate the background against which movies and TV shows are shot. Set illustrators find work through art directors.

Sign Painter (RAE)

Sign painters paint letters and images, usually for businesses. Using their knowledge of typography and design, they draw and measure and use special equipment to produce letters, choosing paint or another medium depending on the surface and location of the sign. They may custom-design letters.

Silkscreen Artist (ARE)

Silkscreen artists create decorative images for posters, clothing, and a variety of other materials. After designing layouts, they prepare silkscreen frames and then print either by hand or machine. Silkscreen artists are employed by commercial silkscreen companies and by manufacturers who have in-house silkscreen departments.

Stained-Glass Artist (ASE) ➡

Stained-glass artists create original designs for art objects and windows made of stained glass. They consult with clients, study the surrounding architecture, and integrate practical requirements with knowledge of glass cutting and symbolic imagery. After drawing the design and estimating cost, they make a full-size working pattern and select and cut glass according to the pattern. They may assemble the pieces, secure them in place, paint or stain the glass and fire it to stabilize the colors, and install the finished window. Stained-glass artists freelance and are hired by stained-glass studios, churches, and businesses.

Stylist (ARE)

Stylists improve the appearance of their subject. For example, **food stylists** arrange food before it is photographed for magazines and cookbooks. **Fashion stylists** prepare models' clothing, accessories, and makeup for photographic shoots and fashion shows. **Hair stylists** add style to a haircut. **Automobile stylists** make sketches to depict the appearance of a new car, including interior and exterior views as well as part and whole views. **House stylists** give houses a particular look, such as Craftsman or French Country. Stylists are employed by individuals, art directors, photographers, modeling agencies, industrial design firms, and manufacturers.

Technical Illustrator (ARI) ➡

Technical illustrators lay out and draw illustrations dealing with the assembly, installation, operation, maintenance, and repair of machines, tools, and equipment. Their drawings and views show the function and relationship of parts and the sequence to be followed in assembly. They may color or shade parts of the illustration to emphasize certain features. Technical illustrators are hired by engineering firms, manufacturing firms, and publishers of technical manuals and reference works. The median annual wage in 2013 was $62,000.

PHOTOGRAPHERS

Camera Operator (AES)

Camera operators take photographs using film, TV broadcasting, or video cameras and equipment. They may set up and operate equipment such as dollies, cranes, and power zooms. During filming they monitor and solve problems related to exposure, movement, and distance. They may maintain their equipment and perform minor repairs. Some camera operators specialize in a particular field, such as news, commercials, cartoons, or medicine. Camera operators specializing in film are also called motion picture photographers. Camera operators are employed by TV stations or film studios. Other employers include independent production firms, advertising agencies, corporate media centers, the government, hospitals and laboratories, and educational institutions. The median annual wage in 2013 was $42,530.

Director of Photography (AES) ➡

Directors of photography, also known as cinematographers, plan and direct the filming of motion pictures. After learning about the cinematic effects desired by the director, they look over the set or location and determine the lighting and photographic equipment needed. They choose camera angles, depth of focus, and so on; select appropriate equipment; and then instruct the camera crew in setting up cameras at the proper distance. During filming, they observe lighting, make adjustments, and signal the beginning and end of filming. After filming, they review the film to see if further adjustments need to be made. Some directors of photography specialize in filming special effects. They are employed by film producers and directors.

Photojournalist (AEC) ➡

Photojournalists photograph newsworthy subjects with still cameras. They travel to an assigned location to take pictures, later processing their film or files and turning their images over to an editor. Photojournalists are employed by print media, including newspapers, magazines, and other journals. Some freelance. The median annual wage in 2013 was $43,000.

Still Photographer (ARS) ➡

Still photographers use still cameras to photograph a variety of subjects. They choose appropriate equipment, plan a composition, position the camera and subject, measure light and distance or create their own light, adjust lens aperture and shutter speed, and take pictures. Some photographers develop their own pictures and may touch up negatives or prints; they may manipulate digital images and scanned prints and film on a computer. Photographers may specialize in areas such as portraits, weddings, fashion, law enforcement, nature, or architecture. Portrait studios and commercial photography studios employ photographers, as do newspapers, magazines, advertising agencies, hospitals, crime labs, and the government. Almost half of U.S. photographers are self-employed. They may contract work to the above employers, run a portrait photography business, or sell photos to stock photo services. The median annual wage in 2013 was $29,280.

PERFORMERS

Instrumental Musician (ASI) ➡

Instrumental musicians perform as soloists or as members of a band or orchestra or other musical group. In addition to playing music, they may also compose, improvise, or transpose. **Session musicians** play background music for a singer in a recording studio. **Accompanists** are instrumental musicians who accompany other musicians. Instrumental musicians are hired by professional orchestras and symphonies; chamber music groups; recording companies; producers of ballet, musicals, opera, films, and TV shows or commercials; churches and synagogues; clubs, cruise ships, theme parks, and restaurants; and planners of weddings and other social or cultural events. The median hourly wage in 2013 was $23.74.

Laserist (ASI) ➡

Laserists create optical shows to entertain audiences, projecting laser designs that are accompanied by music. They also maintain optical and sound equipment, testing and repairing equipment as necessary. Laserists work at planetariums and amusement parks and for producers of packaged laser shows. They may also freelance.

Magician (AES) ➡

Magicians perform sleight-of-hand tricks using props such as rabbits, scarves, and cards to create illusions that mystify and entertain an audience. Corporations sometimes hire magicians to deliver a product message at trade shows, sales meetings, and hospitality suites. Magicians also find work through cruise lines, theme parks, entertainment agencies, and event-planning services, and appear at restaurants, nightclubs, private parties, and banquets.

Puppeteer (AEI) ➡

Puppeteers create puppet shows: they come up with an idea for a show, write an original script or adaptation of a story, design and construct puppets for each role, and then animate them during performance, giving them a voice through talking or singing or operating audio equipment. Puppeteers most commonly make hand, string, shadow, or rod puppets; some use animatronic devices. Puppeteers work for puppet companies, children's theaters and children's museums, TV stations, and amusement parks. Self-employed puppeteers may entertain at school assemblies, company picnics, and birthday parties, also finding work through entertainment agencies and event-planning services.

ELECTRONIC DESIGNERS

Cable Television Program Director (EAS)

Cable TV program directors work at cable TV stations, operating video equipment and coordinating the work of employees who select and produce cable TV programs. They hire workers and instruct them in maintenance and operation of TV equipment. They write scripts and rehearse them with entertainers, coordinating the scripts with sound, music, and visuals to produce shows. When filming and editing a program, they operate cameras, sound mixers, video decks, and other equipment. Cable TV program directors also prepare budgets and perform public-relations functions, such as writing press releases. In 2013, the median annual wage for a program director in the television industry was $69,480.

Film or Video Editor (AES) ➡

Film editors use film splicers to edit film; analog and digital video editors use editing equipment to edit video recordings and soundtracks. After selecting and cutting segments based on their visual appeal as well as their educational or entertainment value, editors reassemble segments to achieve continuity and dramatic effect. Some editors specialize in areas such as news, music, animation, sound effects, and electronic graphics. Film and video editors work for producers of motion pictures, motion picture studios, TV stations, cable companies, independent production companies, production and postproduction facilities, corporate television centers, media centers, and advertising agencies. The median annual wage in 2013 was $54,490.

Game Designer (ARE) ➡

Game designers combine art with computer software to create original electronic games. They create an exciting user experience with a core concept that includes rules of play, challenging obstacles, and characters taking action against a unique backdrop. Game designers are employed by game companies whose products may be played on handheld devices, home systems, or arcade machines. The median annual wage for a video game designer in 2013 was $82,340.

Media Production Specialist (AES) ➡

Media production specialists use audiovisual technology to produce educational materials. When planning video productions, they coordinate the work of writers, designers, and actors. They arrange for settings and props before directing the production. Some set up and run cameras and other media equipment. Media production specialists are employed by corporations, nonprofits, educational institutions, video and film production companies, advertising agencies, TV stations and networks, and the government.

Multimedia Designer (AER) ➡

Multimedia designers integrate multiple media—such as audio, text, video, and animation—to create interactive and nonlinear digital products. Specialties include graphic design, information and user interface design, instructional design, sound design, and website design. Multimedia designers are employed by digital media companies, training firms, advertising firms, companies with in-house multimedia departments, and organizations with Internet or intranet websites. They may also freelance. In 2013, multimedia artists and animators earned median wages of $30.99 hourly and $64,470 annually.

Online Content Developer (AIR) ➡

Online content developers research, write, design, and edit information that is published online. They create text and graphics for online services, bulletin boards, and websites. Content developers work for new media companies, online content production studios, electronic publishers, and organizations that maintain intranet or Internet websites, as well as more traditional employers such as magazines, public-relations firms, and advertising agencies.

Software Designer (IAR) ➡

Software designers create software programs that tell computers what to do. For example, a software designer developed the electronic spreadsheet. Software designers are responsible for the conception and usability of a software product, from its overall structure to the details on the command menu. Software designers are employed by software development companies. Median wages for software developers (and other computer software applications engineers) in 2013 were $44.55 hourly and $92,660 annually.

Special-Effects Artist (ARS) ➡

Special-effects artists work with digital multimedia to produce special effects that are otherwise impossible or very difficult to achieve. They create images and sound effects that buttress the story in a film or other dramatic production, including commercials, trailers, and games. Special-effects artists are employed in FX (special effects) studios, motion picture and TV studios, postproduction houses, game companies, and special effects boutique companies.

Television Technician (ASI) ➡

Television technicians perform a variety of duties both in and outside the TV studio. Their duties include operating studio cameras or portable cameras; operating video consoles to transmit TV scenes; producing films or videos for educational and training purposes; and setting up and operating other equipment used for TV broadcasting, such as lights, microphones, and recording systems. Television technicians also maintain their equipment and perform minor repairs. Median wages in 2013 were $17.65 hourly and $36,710 annually.

Webcomic Artist (AER) ➡

Webcomic artists produce comic strips and post them online. They develop characters and dialogue as well as draw comic strips in their own style, in either one-shot or serial form. They may also interact with their fans via email or social media. Webcomic artists who have achieved a large enough following make income from advertisements and from the sale of their original products, such as T-shirts and comic books.

SUPERVISORS

Art Director (AES) ➡

Art directors formulate persuasive concepts to be presented by visual communications media and supervise workers who prepare art layouts. After reviewing the material to be presented and learning the clients' objectives and constraints, they formulate basic design concepts and select illustrations. They may prepare art design layouts themselves or assign staff members to do so. They then review, approve, and present final layouts to the client. Art directors work in advertising agencies, in-house advertising departments, and publishing companies. The median annual wage in 2013 was $83,000.

Display Manager (AES) ➡

Display managers develop interior advertising displays and supervise workers who lay out and assemble them. After consulting with advertising and salespeople to learn when and where particular merchandise is to be displayed, they develop layouts that integrate theme, color, light, and props. They then order necessary materials and oversee construction. Display managers work for retail establishments and display houses that produce displays for showrooms, special events, and trade shows.

Film or Video Editor Supervisor (EAS) ➡

Supervising film or video editors supervise and coordinate the work of employees who edit and assemble sequences of prerecorded film or video. After studying the script and conferring with producers and directors, they review the film or video, correct errors, trim sequences to appropriate length, and assemble segments in a sequence that achieves the desired effects. Supervising film or video editors may be employed by motion picture studios, motion picture producers, TV stations, cable companies, independent production companies, production and postproduction facilities, corporate television centers, media centers, and advertising agencies.

Multimedia Director (EAS) ➡

Multimedia directors collaborate to create a vision for a multimedia product and then direct and integrate the work of artists, writers, and programmers to complete the product on time and within budget. Larger companies may have a producer, creative director, art director, technical director, and video director all working with each other; in smaller companies, one person plays several roles simultaneously. Multimedia directors are employed by digital media companies, corporations and companies with in-house multimedia departments, training firms, and advertising firms. They also freelance.

Scenic Arts Supervisor (AES)

Scenic arts supervisors create layouts of scenery and backdrops and supervise artists who paint them. After consulting with the art director, they prepare sketches and estimate the materials and labor needed as well as the cost of supplies in order to prepare a budget. Scenic arts supervisors work in film and TV sound stages; some find work through art directors.

Suspect Artist Supervisor (ASE)

Suspect artist supervisors work for law enforcement agencies in very large cities, coordinating the activities of workers who form composite images of criminal suspects. Like the artists they train and supervise, they also arrange and enhance sets of facial features to form composite images.

FINISHERS

Body-Makeup Artist (AER)

Body-makeup artists apply makeup to the bodies of performers so that their bodies will match their faces in tone and texture. After preparing grease paint or liquid makeup of the desired shade, they use fingers or sponge to apply it to exposed areas of the performer's body. Body-makeup artists are hired by costume designers, theater groups, makeup companies, individual entertainers, and producers of entertainment.

Calligrapher (ARE)

Using a variety of pens, brushes, paint, and ink, calligraphers hand-letter, embellish, and decorate diplomas, testimonials, citations, and other documents. **Illuminators** are calligraphers that design and draw initial letters, scrollwork, and borders for books and posters. Calligraphers may freelance to a variety of organizations, such as advertising agencies, public-relations firms, design firms, cultural and civic agencies, and special-events planners.

Copyist (AES)

Apparel manufacturing firms hire copyists to gather information on fashion trends and sketch detailed examples of clothing made by competitors. Copyists attend fashion shows, review fashion magazines, read trade publications, and talk to people in the garment industry to learn about new trends, consumer preferences, and price ranges.

Costumer (ARI)

Costumers work for producers of motion pictures and television shows, selecting and fitting costumes for cast members. After analyzing the script, they study books and pictures to determine the styles worn at that particular time and place in history. They select costumes from the stock they have inventoried, examine the costumes on the cast member, make minor alterations and repairs by hand, and send major alterations to the tailor. The median annual wage for a costumer in 2013 was $36,650.

Drafter (RAC)

Drafters take rough sketches from architects, industrial designers, and engineers, turning them into detailed drawings that contain information needed for building and manufacturing. Using computer-aided design (CAD) or conventional drafting tools, they analyze specifications and calculations to refine a three-dimensional image and graphically present plans. Drafters are employed by architects, design firms, and manufacturing industries. Median wages in 2013 were about $22.92 hourly and $47,680 annually.

Engraver (RAC)

Engravers are employed by engraving companies to lay out and engrave or carve letters and designs on the surface of metal and other materials such as glassware or plastic, using handheld power tools. They may also suggest and sketch original designs. Median wages in 2013 were $13.70 hourly and $28,510 annually.

Exhibit Artist (ASI)

Exhibit artists work for museums and zoos and similar establishments, producing artwork for permanent or temporary exhibits. After learning about the purpose of the exhibit and the type of artwork desired, they make scale drawings and follow the designer's layout. They paint a background and prepare photographs as well as titles and legends and accessories to complete the exhibit's design.

Fabric and Apparel Patternmaker (RAC)

Fabric and apparel patternmakers draw master patterns for use in constructing garments. They convert a model garment into pattern pieces that can be cut and assembled from a length of fabric. Using tools such as computers and drafting instruments, they create master patterns in a range of sizes and mark pattern pieces with information such as pattern number, sewing instructions, and location of features like buttons and pockets. They may construct sample garments to test fit. Fabric and apparel patternmakers are employed by pattern companies, clothing manufacturers, apparel wholesalers, textile mills, and clothing designers. In 2013, median wages were $40,130.

Foley Artist (ARE)

Foley artists work for TV and movie studios to create sounds that accompany onscreen images. After reviewing cue sheets to learn the sequence of movements in a scene, they produce custom sounds to replace physical sounds that were lost because microphones focus on dialogue. Foley artists get into character, timing their use of props to match sounds with actions like starting a car or stepping on glass. Their sounds are recorded and then sent to the director for approval. Wages for less experienced foley artists outside the union were $200 a day in 2010; more experienced foley artist in the union, between $340 to $450 a day.

Furniture Finisher (RAE)

Furniture finishers repair and refinish used furniture as well as shape and finish new furniture. After examining the furniture to determine the best approach, they choose from a variety of tools, such as wood putty and sandpaper, and finishes such as stain and oil, applying them to repair worn or damaged furniture or achieve a specific color or finish on new furniture. Furniture finishers are employed by manufacturers of household furniture, office furniture, and kitchen cabinets, and also by furniture stores and furniture repair shops. In 2013, median wages were $28,470. Many furniture finishers are self-employed.

Glass Decorator (RAE)

Glass decorators work for glass manufacturers, etching or cutting artistic designs in glass articles. They decorate bowls, vases, stemware, and other items by using acid solutions and sandblasting equipment.

Hand-Painter (RAC)

Hand-painters work for manufacturers in any industry, decorating objects such as pottery, glassware, china, buttons, and notions. They may sketch a design first, follow a model, or paint freehand. After grinding colors, they mix them with oils and apply paint with hand brushes.

Jewelry Crafter (ARE)

Jewelry crafters follow drawings or instructions to make sample jewelry for accessories manufacturing firms. Using metal cutting and shaping tools, they cut and shape metal, softening metal findings with a gas torch and soldering pieces together according to jewelry design. They smooth and polish rough surfaces and attach stones and other decorative trimmings.

Milliner (AES)

Milliners make hats for retail stores, cutting material to follow an original pattern or copying the design of an existing hat. Using hat forms and a steam iron, they mold, drape, and block material and then sew it together, trimming it with flowers, veils, ribbons, and other decorations. Milliners may also alter hats or make custom hats for customers.

Painting Instructor (AES)

Painting instructors work for retailers, indirectly promoting sales by teaching ornamental painting. They select plaques and fabrics and other materials for customers, demonstrate painting techniques, and give advice on purchases.

Photography Colorist (AEC)

Colorists work for photography studios, applying oil colors to portrait photographs to produce a natural, lifelike appearance. Using cotton swabs and brushes, they apply photographic colors freehand, wiping off excess and blending into the photograph to produce the desired effect.

Pottery Manufacturer (RAC)

Manufacturers of pottery employ potters to operate machines such as jigger machines and pug mills, processing clay to produce pottery products, including stoneware and ceramics. In 2013, median wages for manufacturing potters were $29,790.

Precious Metal Worker (RAC)

Precious metals include gold, silver, pewter, and platinum. Precious metal workers use those metals to form household items, such as serving trays and candlesticks. Using a variety of tools, such as hammers and blowtorches, they cast, cut, solder, engrave, and polish metal, shaping the piece to specifications. They may be self-employed or work for retail trade or manufacturers of precious metal products. In 2013, median wages for precious metal workers were $35,520.

Renderer (RAI)

Renderers (also called delineators) prepare perspective drawings of interiors or exteriors of buildings. After listening to the ideas of clients and architects and interior designers, and possibly consulting blueprints or layouts, they illustrate how the completed building or furnished interior will look. Architectural and interior renderers are employed by architecture and interior design firms or freelance to clients, architects, and interior designers.

Sound Engineering Technician (RAE)

Sound engineering technicians operate equipment to record and reproduce sounds, including music and voices. They may set up microphones and other recording equipment, make adjustments for volume and sound quality, and later edit, mix, separate and/or combine sounds. Technicians at radio and television studios may produce artificial sounds in synchrony with the broadcast. Technicians in live concert settings help musicians achieve their desired sound and impact. Sound-effects technicians are employed at sporting arenas, recording studios, radio and TV stations, and video and film production companies. Median wages in 2013 were $46,480.

Stained-Glass Glazier (ARI)

Stained-glass glaziers follow an already-designed pattern (that may have been created by a stained-glass artist), selecting and cutting colored glass for use in stained-glass windows in churches, memorials, and residences. They select glass of the proper color, cut it with a glass cutter, and then assemble the stained glass by soldering joints of lead stripping between the glass pieces. They may repair stained-glass windows and lamp shades. Stained-glass glaziers may freelance or work for stained-glass studios, memorial studios, or churches.

Stone Carver (RAE)

Stone carvers carve designs and figures in full and bas-relief on stone. Following a designer's sketch, blueprint, or model, they transfer the dimensions of the design onto the stone's surface. Using chisels and pneumatic tools, they rough out the design and then further shape, trim, and smooth the stone. Stone carvers are employed by memorial studios, monument companies, the larger quarries and fabricators of granite, and contractors who build stone edifices.

Suspect Artist (ASE)

Working from information provided by the victim of (or a witness to) a crime, suspect artists assemble images of possible suspects, using a kit or, increasingly, a computer program, modifying them until the interviewee is satisfied that the image resembles the suspect. They also search police records for possible matches.

Tattoo Artist (AEC)

Tattoo artists apply tattoos to the skin of customers. After shaving and washing the area that will receive the tattoo, they trace a stencil or draw an outline of the design onto the skin, then apply ink using an electric tattoo gun. Between customers they sterilize needles, mix pigments, repair tools, and create original designs. Tattoo artists work in tattoo shops or salons. Many are self-employed.

Wallcovering Texturer (RAS)

Wallcovering texturers work for wallpaper manufacturers, dripping or sponging paint in a specified pattern to create texture. Consulting the product card and paint sample book, they apply the specified color in the manner and pattern prescribed.

MODEL BUILDERS

Brick and Tile Modeler (ARI)

Modelers mold original designs, such as fountains and waterspouts, in decorative tile. They cut and scrape and finish plaster of paris to sculpture a model, sometimes constructing a wooden mold to cast clay models. Modelers work on commission to individuals or organizations. Some are employed by manufacturers of brick and tile products.

Concrete Sculptor (RAI)

Concrete sculptors construct models and molds for manufacturers of concrete garden furniture and statuary. They build a metal framework, model clay according to drawings or pictures, brush layers of rubber paint onto their clay model to form a cast, and then cover the cast with a shield of fiberglass, which they later remove, reassemble, and fill with concrete.

Exhibit Builder (ARS)

Exhibit builders work for museums, constructing exhibit structures and installing electric wiring and other fixtures in the framework. They study sketches to determine materials needed and use hand tools and power tools to construct the framework and its components. They finish the structure by applying paint or texture, affixing murals or photographs, and mounting legends or graphics. Once the exhibit is assembled and installed, they test mechanical and electrical components.

Glassblower (RAE)

Glassblowers design, blow, and shape glass for laboratory apparatus such as test tubes, flasks, thermometers, condensers, and vacuum pumps. Knowing the effects of heat and chemicals, they develop specifications and design custom glass products. Laboratory apparatus glassblowers are employed by universities, research labs, and glass manufacturers.

Miniature-Set Constructor (ARE)

Miniature-set constructors build miniature models of motion picture sets for filming backgrounds, titles, and special effects. They cut and fit building materials with hand tools to form three-dimensional set pieces. After forming landscapes and foliage, they trim and paint the completed set. Miniature-set constructors are employed by production designers and postproduction facilities. They may find work through art directors.

Model Maker (ARI)

Model makers work for industries such as ship or boat builders or automobile manufacturers, building production models to scale. Using materials such as wood, fiberglass, or metal, they construct a scale model of the object to be manufactured. Some model makers build miniature models of buildings or redevelopment projects for architects or city governments; some build prototypes for industrial designers.

Pottery and Porcelain Model Maker (RAE)

Model makers work for manufacturers of pottery and porcelain, constructing models of pieces that will be used for casting molds.

Working with plaster, clay, or both, they shape it with their hands or shave it with steel-cutting tools as it revolves on the spinning table.

Property Maker (ARS)

Property makers work for theaters, making stage props and sets look authentic to the theater audience. They transform everyday materials (fabric, wood, wire, paper, and the like) into fake products (such as stairs, marble hallways, jewel-studded crowns) using hand tools and machinery.

Stage Technician (ARS)

Stage technicians erect stages and install rigging, lighting, scenery, and sound equipment. They consult the stage manager and blueprints; assemble sets, props, and scenery; position lighting and sound equipment; and connect electrical wiring. During rehearsal and performance, they operate lighting and sound equipment and pull cables to raise and lower curtains and scenery. Stage technicians are employed by theaters and production companies. Some work in arenas, stadiums, and amusement parks. The median annual wage in 2013 was $41,250.

FOOD PREPARERS

Cake Decorator (ARE)

Cake decorators decorate pastries and cakes. After trimming and cutting the cake to a desired shape, they spread frosting, tint icing, and squeeze it out of a bag while designing decorations. Cake decorators work in retail bakeries and retail eating places, grocery stores, and institutional kitchens. The median annual wage for a cake decorator in 2013 was $20,000.

Chef (EAR)

Chefs supervise and coordinate cooks and other kitchen workers who prepare foods for customers. Some chefs also plan and develop recipes and menus and create decorative food displays. They order and check quality and quantity of incoming foods and may teach staff new cooking techniques as well as do some cooking themselves. Chefs are employed by hotels, resorts, cruise ships, restaurants, and private clients. Personal chefs may go to clients' homes to prepare entrées and side dishes, earning more than $50,000 annually. Median wages for chefs and head cooks in 2013 were $20.43 hourly and $42,490 annually.

Chef de Froid (RAE)

Chefs de froid design decorations for food and create artistic arrangements of food for formal buffets. They prepare and decorate foods like hors d'oeuvres and relishes, mold butter into decorative shapes, sculpt ice, carve meat, and arrange fruits and vegetables. Chefs de froid usually work in formal restaurants, including those in hotels and country clubs and cruise ships. Other employers are cooking schools and caterers for movie companies and special events.

Dairy Products Decorator (AES)

Dairy products decorators mold and decorate ice cream confections using spatulas, stencils, spray guns, and whipped cream dispensers. Dairy products decorators are employed by ice cream and frozen yogurt establishments, large hotels, cruise ships, restaurants serving gourmet desserts, and caterers serving the media. The median hourly wage for special food services cooks in 2013 was $9.57.

Ice Cream Chef (RAS)

Ice cream chefs make and decorate ice cream, sherbets, and other frozen desserts with sauces and syrups. Ice cream chefs work in restaurants, ice cream parlors, and ice cream production companies. The median hourly wage for special food services cooks in 2013 was $9.57.

Pastry Chef (EAR)

Pastry chefs are supervisors who coordinate the activities of the workers who prepare desserts, confections, and pastries, although some may also prepare such items themselves. They plan dessert menus, order supplies, and supervise production. Pastry chefs work for restaurants, hotels, government and factory cafeterias, grocery stores, bakeries, and institutional kitchens. The median annual salary for bakers in 2013 was $23,160.

Pastry Cook (RAS)

Pastry cooks prepare cakes, cookies, custards, pies, puddings, and other desserts, which they may decorate with toppings, icings, and ornaments. Pastry cooks work in restaurants, hotels, government and factory cafeterias, grocery stores, bakery shops, and the kitchens of nursing homes, hospitals, and educational institutions.

RESTORERS

Antiques Specialist (EAR)

Antiques specialists specialize in historical furnishings and accessories for interior design. They locate, buy, restore, and then sell antiques to private clients and interior designers. Some antiques specialists may also freelance as consultants or appraisers.

Ceramic Restorer (ASI)

Ceramic restorers work for museums, cleaning, preserving, and restoring ceramic ware. They recommend preservation measures to prevent damage or deterioration, and they repair broken wares to reproduce their original appearance. Ceramic restorers also construct replicas of ceramic ware, basing their design on existing remnants and their knowledge of ceramic history.

Musical Instrument Repairer and Tuner (RAI)

Musical instrument repairers adjust and repair instruments that are damaged or broken. After inspecting and playing the instrument to pinpoint problems, they disassemble it, repair or replace parts, and reassemble it, playing it to make sure it's fixed. They may need to create and build new parts for older instruments. Musical instrument tuners may only tune the instrument and may specialize in a single instrument, such as piano tuning. Some repairers specialize according to type of instrument, such as reed, string, keyboard, or percussion. Musical instrument repairers work for music stores, factories, repair shops, schools, and museums. Some are self-employed. Median annual wages in 2013 were $31,750.

Paintings Conservator (ASR)

Paintings conservators preserve and restore paintings that are faded or damaged. They research and examine a painting and test its surface to select appropriate cleaning solvents, then clean the surface and apply paint where needed, blending their work to maintain the style of the original. In addition to preservation, they may plan the care of an entire collection. Paintings conservators are hired by museums, institutions with painting collections, regional conservation centers, historical sites and houses, and private collectors. Some are self-employed. The median annual wage in 2013 was $40,020.

Paper and Prints Restorer (AIS)

Paper-and-prints restorers work for libraries and museums, cleaning, preserving, restoring, and repairing paper objects of historic and artistic importance. After they examine the book, document, map, print, or photograph to identify the problem, they plan and execute the safest and most effective treatment. The median annual wage in 2013 was $40,020.

———

In addition to the *Dictionary of Occupational Titles* and the United States Department of Labor's O*Net OnLine and Bureau of Labor Statistics, the following references were used in assembling this appendix:

Bly, Robert. *Careers for Writers and Others Who Have a Way with Words*, 2nd ed. Chicago: VGM Career Books, 2003.

Brommer, Gerald, and Joseph Gatto. *Careers in Art: An Illustrated Guide*, 2nd ed. Worcester, MA: Davis Publications, 1999.

Eberts, Marjorie, and Margaret Gisler. *Careers for Bookworms and Other Literary Types*, 3rd ed. Chicago: VGM Career Books, 2002.

———. *Careers for Culture Lovers and Other Artsy Types*, 2nd ed. Chicago: VGM Career Horizons, 1999.

Field, Shelly. *Career Opportunities in the Music Industry*, 3rd ed. New York: Facts on File, 1995.

———. *Career Opportunities in Theater and the Performing Arts*. New York: Facts on File, 1992.

———. *100 Best Careers for Writers and Artists*. New York: Arco, 1998.

Goldberg, Jan. *Careers for Class Clowns and Other Engaging Types*, 2nd ed. Chicago: McGraw-Hill, 2005.

Guiley, Rosemary. *Career Opportunities for Writers*, 2nd ed. New York: Facts on File, 1991.

Mauro, Lucia. *Careers for Fashion Plates and Other Trendsetters*, 2nd ed. Chicago: VGM Career Books, 2003.

Maze, Marilyn, and Donald Mayall, comps. *The Enhanced Guide for Occupational Exploration: Descriptions for the 2,800 Most Important Jobs*, 2nd ed. Indianapolis: JIST Works, Inc., 1995.

Public Affairs Coalition of the Alliance of Motion Picture and Television Producers. *Making Digits Dance: Visual Effects and Animation Careers in the Entertainment Industry*. Los Angeles: North Valley Private Industry Council, 1997.

Regan and Associates. *A Labor Market Analysis of the Interactive Digital Media Industry: Opportunities in Multimedia*. Los Angeles: North Valley Private Industry Council, 1997.

NOTES

1. Gallup, "State of the American Workplace Report, 2013," www.gallup.com/strategicconsulting/163007/state-american-workplace.aspx (accessed June, 2014).

2. Rich Feller and Judy Whichard, *Knowledge Nomads and the Nervously Employed: Workplace Change & Courageous Career Choices* (Austin, TX: CAPS Press, 2005), 11–12.

3. John Holland, *Making Vocational Choices: A Theory of Vocational Personalities and Work Environments*, 3rd ed. (Odessa, FL: Psychological Assessment Resources, 1997).

4. Daniel Pink, *A Whole New Mind: Moving from the Information Age to the Conceptual Age* (New York: Riverhead Books, 2005), 55.

5. Virginia Postrel, *The Substance of Style: How the Rise of Aesthetic Value Is Remaking Commerce, Culture, and Consciousness* (New York: HarperCollins, 2003).

6. Richard Florida, *The Rise of the Creative Class: And How It's Transforming Work, Leisure, Community, and Everyday Life* (New York: Basic Books, 2002).

7. B. Joseph Pine II and James Gilmore, *The Experience Economy: Work Is Theatre and Every Business a Stage* (Boston: Harvard Business School Press, 1999), 3.

8. Stuart Cunningham, "Developments in Measuring the 'Creative' Workforce," *Cultural Trends*, vol. 20, no. 1 (March 2011): 25–40.

9. Roberta Comunian, Alessandra Faggian, and Qian Cher Li, "Unrewarded Careers in the Creative Class: The Strange Case of Bohemian Graduates," *Papers in Regional Science*, vol. 89, issue 2 (June 2010): 389–410.

10. *California's Entertainment Workforce: Employment and Earnings 1991–2002* (Pacific Palisades, CA: The Entertainment Economy Institute and The PMR Group, 2004).

11. Cunningham, "Developments in Measuring the 'Creative' Workforce," 28.

12. John Wright, *The American Almanac of Jobs and Salaries*, 2000–2001 ed. (New York: Avon Books, 2000).

13. John French et al., *Career Change in Midlife: Stress, Social Support, and Adjustment* (Ann Arbor, MI: University of Michigan, 1983).

14. John French et al., *The Mechanisms of Job Stress and Strain* (New York: Wiley, 1982).

15. If you are curious about media anthropology, I recommend that you read my friend Susan's book: Susan Allen, ed., *Media Anthropology: Informing Global Citizens* (Westport, CT: Gergin & Garvey, 1994).

16. Yoash Weiner, Yoav Vardi, and Jan Muczyk, "Antecedents of Employees' Mental Health—The Role of Career and Work Satisfaction," *Journal of Vocational Behavior*, no. 19 (1981): 50–60.

17. James O'Toole, *Work in America: Report of a Special Task Force to the Secretary of Health, Education, and Welfare* (Cambridge, MA: MIT Press, 1973).

18. Colin Martindale, "What Makes Creative People Different?" *Psychology Today*, July 1975, 44–46, 97–98.

19. Georgia O'Keefe, "About Myself," in *Georgia O'Keefe: Exhibition of Oils and Pastels* (New York: An American Place, 1939).

20. I am grateful to Betty Comtois for the original expression of these ideas.

21. Donald MacKinnon, *In Search of Human Effectiveness* (Buffalo, NY: Creative Education Foundation, 1978), 47.

22. Steven Hayes, Kirk Strosahl, and Kelly Wilson, *Acceptance and Commitment Therapy: The Process and Practice of Mindful Change*, 2nd ed. (New York: Guildford Press, 2012).

23. E. Craven, *The Use of Interest Inventories in Counseling* (Chicago: Science Research Associates, 1961).

24. J. Getzels and Mihaly Csikszentmihalyi, *The Creative Vision: A Longitudinal Study of Problem Finding in Art* (New York: Wiley Interscience, 1976), 22.

25. Richard Nelson Bolles, *What Color Is Your Parachute? A Practical Manual for Job-Hunters & Career Changers*, 2015 ed. (Berkeley, CA: Ten Speed Press, 2014).

26. Richard Nelson Bolles, *What Color Is Your Parachute? Job-Hunter's Workbook*, 4th ed. (Berkeley, CA: Ten Speed Press, 2012).

27. Arthur Miller and Ralph Mattson, *The Truth about You* (Berkeley, CA: Ten Speed Press, 1989).

28. This good idea was suggested to me by one of my readers in London, Louise Vale.

29. Alvin Toffler, *Powershift: Knowledge, Wealth, and Violence at the Edge of the 21st Century* (New York: Bantam Books, 1990), 82.

30. Florida, *Rise of the Creative Class*, 69.

31. Ibid., 8.

32. Roberta Comunian, Alessandra Faggian, and Sarah Jewell, "Winning and Losing in the Creative Industries: An Analysis of Creative Graduates' Career Opportunities Across Creative Disciplines," *Cultural Trends*, vol. 20, nos. 3–4 (September–December 2011): 291–308.

33. Cunningham, "Developments in Measuring the 'Creative' Workforce," 25–40.

34. Chris Anderson, *Makers: The New Industrial Revolution* (New York: Crown Business, 2012), 66.

35. Gary Gottfredson and John Holland, *Dictionary of Holland Occupational Codes*, 3rd ed. (Odessa, FL: Psychological Assessment Resources, 1996).

36. Donald Clifton, Edward Anderson, and Laurie Schreiner, *Strengths Quest: Discover and Develop Your Strengths in Academics, Career, and Beyond*, 2nd ed. (New York: Gallup Press, 2006).

37. Patty Azzarello, *Rise: 3 Practical Steps for Advancing Your Career, Standing Out as a Leader, and Liking Your Life* (Berkeley, CA: Ten Speed Press, 2012), 52.

38. Freelancers Union, 2011, "America's Uncounted Independent Workforce," www.fu-res.org/pdfs/advocacy/2011_Counting_the_Independent_Workforce%20Policy_Brief.pdf (accessed August, 2014).

39. Howard Figler, *The Complete Job Search Handbook* (New York: Henry Holt, 1988), 219.

40. Deborah Jacobsen, *150 Jobs You Can Start Today: Creative Ways to Make Money Now* (New York: Broadway Books, 2003).

41. Elizabeth W. Brewer, *Vocational Souljourn Paradigm*, unpublished manuscript, 1996.

42. Rollo May, *The Courage to Create* (New York: Bantam Books, 1975), 134.

43. Barbara Sher, *Wishcraft: How to Get What You Really Want* (New York: Ballantine Books, 1979).

44. Barbara Sher, *I Could Do Anything If I Only Knew What It Was* (New York: Delacorte Press, 1994).

45. I am indebted to one of my readers, Camila Gaddy, who generously shared her ideas and enthusiasm regarding a career notebook, and to my colleague from the 1990s, Marti Moore, who recommended similar ideas.

46. Russ Harris, *ACT Made Simple: An Easy to Read Primer on Acceptance and Commitment Therapy* (Oakland, CA: New Harbinger Publications, 2009), 207.

47. David Burns, *Feeling Good: The New Mood Therapy* (New York: Signet, 1980), 333–34.

48. Dennis Kelly and Karen Peterson, "Success Not Defined in Dollars and Cents," *USA Today*, September 25, 1995.

49. Julia Cameron, *The Artist's Way: A Spiritual Path to Higher Creativity* (Los Angeles: J. P. Tarcher, 1992).

50. Ronald Finke, Thomas Ward, and Steven Smith, *Creative Cognition: Theory, Research, and Practice* (Cambridge, MA: MIT Press, 1996), 35.

51. Benjamin Bloom, "The Role of Gifts and Markers in the Development of Talent," *Exceptional Children*, vol. 48, no. 6 (April 1982): 510–22.

52. William Bridges, *Transitions: Making Sense of Life's Changes* (New York: Addison-Wesley, 1980), 103.

53. Ibid., 131.

54. Matthew Fox, *Original Blessing: A Primer in Creation Spirituality* (Santa Fe, NM: Bear & Co., 1983), 186.

55. Mihaly Csikszentmihalyi, *Flow: The Psychology of Optimal Experience* (New York: Harper and Row, 1990).

56. D. Schneider, *The Psychoanalyst and the Artist* (East Hampton, NY: Alexa Press, 1979), 140.

57. MacKinnon, *In Search of Human Effectiveness*, 135.

58. P. Mullahy, *Oedipus: Myth and Complex* (New York: Hermitage Press, 1948), 184.

59. Marcus Bach, *The Power of Perfect Liberty* (Englewood Cliffs, NJ: Prentice Hall, 1971), 29–30.

60. Harry Hurt III, *For All Mankind* (New York: Atlantic Monthly Press, 1988), 325–26.

INDEX

Note: Tables are indicated by a letter "t" after the page number

C

cyclical nature of, 147–49
returning with a gift, 145–47
Creative Vision, The, 44–45
Creativity
  essence of, 42
  fears about, 129–130
  finding new outlets for, 148
  honoring, 150–51
  types of, 30, 74–75
  world's need for, 152–55
Critic (AES), 120, 160
Criticism, facing, 146–47
Crossword-puzzle maker (ASE), 160
Crowdfunding, 122–23
Cryptanalyst (IAE), 185
Cue selector (ASE), 166
Curator (EAI), 190–91

D

Dairy products decorator (AES), 247
Dalziel, Michelle, 96–97
Dancer (AER), 171
Dance therapist (ASI), 195
Dancing instruction sales
    representative (EAS), 209–10
Dancing instructor (ASE), 201–2
Dare to Live Your Dream
    (audiotape program), 108
Day jobs
  choosing, 91–92
  for Conventional types, 96–98
  defined, 99
  for Enterprising types, 93–94
  interim jobs, 91–92
  for Investigative types, 94
  job titles, 72
  part-time work, 91–98
  for Realistic types, 94–95
  redesigning your current job, 98–101
  for Social types, 93
  See also Career; Creative
      occupations
Deaf interpreter (ASC), 191
Decision-making process, 5–6

DeGeneres, Ellen, 22
Department editor (AES), 206
Depression, 130, 144
Designers, 212–222, 232–35
Dictionary editor (AIS), 166
*Dictionary of Holland Occupational
    Codes*, 68
Difficulty, anticipating, 117–18
Digital Revolution, 63
Dilbert comic strip, 34, 120
Directors, 164–69
Disc jockey (AES), 171
Display designer (AES), 213–14
Display manager (AES), 236
Double, actor's (AER), 172
Dowley, Carolyn Wadley, 80–81
Drafter (RAC), 238
Drama teacher (ASE), 202
Drucker, Peter, 117
Dylan, Bob, 141

E

Economist (IAS), 65, 176
Editorial writer (AES), 160–61
Education, 43–44
Eiffel Tower, 134
Electronic designers, 232–35
Elementary school teacher (SAI), 202
Eliot, T. S., 92
Ellison, Ralph, 24, 150
English as a second language (ESL)
    Instructor (SAE), 202–3
Engraver (RAC), 239
Enterprising personality, 8t, 10–11, 28t,
    93–94
Entertainers, 208–9
Entrepreneur, 48
Equestrian (AER), 172
Evaluators, 184–87
Exhibit artist, 239
Exhibit builder (ARS), 244–45

Mozart, Amadeus, 133
Multimedia designer (AER), 233–34
Multimedia director (EAS), 236
Music
    director (AES), 167
    instrumental musician (ASI), 230–31
    minister of (ASE), 198
    musical instrument designer
      (ARE), 220
    musical instrument repairer and
      tuner (RAI), 249
    producer (EAS), 167–68
    school music coordinator (EAS)
      183–84
    teacher (AES), 204
    therapist (ASI), 86–87, 196

N

Narrator (AES), 172–73
Negotiators, 197–200
News editor (AES), 168
Newspaper editor (AES), 198–99
"Novel Juggler, The," 79

O

O*NET Ability Profiler (IP), 56
O*NET Interest Profiler (IP), 14, 56
O*NET (Occupational Information
    Network), 69
Occupational Outlook Handbook, 69
O'Keefe, Georgia, 32–33
150 Jobs You Can Start Today, 92–93
Online content developer (AIR), 234
Orchestra conductor (AES), 168
Orchestrator (AEI), 161–62
Ornamental metalwork designer
    (ARS), 220

P

Package designer (AEI), 220–21
Painter (ASI), 225–26
Painting instructor (AES), 241
Paintings conservator (ASR), 249

Paper and prints restorer (AIS), 250
Part-time work, 91–98
Pastry chef (EAR), 248
Pastry cook (RAS), 248
Patent agent (EAI), 186–87
Patron, finding, 80–81
Perfectionism, 114–15
Performers, 169–174, 230–32
Perfumer (IAR), 178
Persistence, 104–5
Personality types, 7–9, 12–15, 20–23
    See also specific types
Persuaders, 209–11
Pewterer (ARS), 225
Philologist (AIS), 178
Photographers, 90–91, 229–230
Photographer's model (AES), 193
Photography colorist (AEC), 241
Photojournalist (AEC), 230
Picasso, Pablo, 133
Pinsky, Carrie, 48
Piotrowski, Katy, 97–98
Playwright (ASE), 162
Poet (AES), 130, 162
Police artist (ASC), 226
Political scientist (IAE), 179
Pottery and porcelain model maker
    (RAE), 245–46
Pottery manufacturer (RAC), 241
Precious metal worker (RAC), 242
Preschool teacher (SAE), 205
Printmaker (AES), 226
Problem-solving, intuitive, 35–37
Program proposals coordinator
    (EAS), 182
Promoters, 187–89
Properties supervisor (EAS), 207
Property maker (ARS), 246
Psychic reader (AEC), 208–9
Psychological Assessment Resources,
    13, 74

Psychological health, 25
Psychotherapist (SAI), 196
Publications editor (AES), 207
Public recognition, 134
Public-relations counselor (EAS), 188
Public-relations specialist (EAS), 188
Puppeteer (AEI), 231–32

Q

Quick-sketch artist (ASE), 226

R

Radio program director (EAS), 182
Rank, Otto, 150
Reader (AES), 162
Realistic personality, 9t, 11, 19, 29t, 44, 94–95
Receptionist (CSE), 18
Records analysis manager (EAI), 182–83
Religious director (EAS), 168–69
Renderer (RAI), 242
Reporter (ASI), 163
Reports analysis manager (EAS), 183
Researcher (IAS), 163
Restorers, 248–250
Ring conductor (EAS), 173
Rowling, J. K., 22

S

Safety-clothing-and-equipment designer (AER), 221
Savickas, Mark, 12
Scenic arts supervisor (AES), 237
School art coordinator (EAS), 183
School music coordinator (EAS), 183–84
Schreiner, Laurie, 74
Screenwriter (AEI), 163
Sculptor (AER), 226
Secondary school teacher (SAE), 205

Self-Directed Search (SDS), 14, 74
Self-esteem, 23, 24, 25, 99, 120
Set decorator (AES), 221
Set illustrator (AES), 227
Sher, Barbara, 92, 108, 121
Show host (EAS), 173
Show operations supervisor (ASE), 207
Siegel, Art, 90–91
Sign painter (RAE), 227
Silkscreen artist (ARE), 227
Singer (AES), 173
Singing messenger (ASC), 209
Skills
    analysis, 54, 56–57
    discovering, 53–62, 66–68
    with information, people and things, 57–59
Skowronek, Jason, 81–82
Small business, running, 87–89
Smith, Dana, 78–79
Social media, 124–28
Social media consultant (EAS), 189
Social personality, 8t, 10, 19, 28t, 44, 93
Social psychologist (IAE), 179
Sociologist (IAE), 179
Socrates, 146
Soderbergh, Steven, 46
Software designer (IAR), 234
Sound designer (ARE), 221
Sound engineering technician (RAE), 242
Special-effects artist (ARS), 234
Speech-language pathologist (SAI), 196–97
Spinoza, 92
Spiritual perspective, 153–54
Stage director (AES), 169
Stage technician (ARS), 246
Stained-glass artist (ASE), 228
Stained-glass glazier (ARI), 243
State arts council, 123–24